YOUR CAREER BREAK

the 'how-to' guide

Sue Hadden

authorHOUSE®

AuthorHouse™
1663 Liberty Drive
Bloomington, IN 47403
www.authorhouse.com
Phone: 1-800-839-8640

Published by AuthorHouse 5/24/2013

ISBN: 978-1-4817-1165-4 (sc)
ISBN: 978-1-4817-1164-7 (e)

Library of Congress Control Number: 2013901829

This book is dedicated to those who have courageously taken a career break or sabbatical to do something they had always dreamed of doing. I hope that the information and ideas in this book encourage you to step out of your daily routine and make the break to do something you're passionate about, and that it makes a difference in your life and the lives of those around you!

TABLE OF CONTENTS

PREFACE

Why Did I Write This Book?

When I told people I was writing this book, they would often say how much they would love a career break and that they needed a book just like this one. This admission often came with a big sigh and a dreamy look. So what is holding them back?

In my experience, one of the biggest hurdles to taking a career break is *fear*. Fear of what will happen to your career, a decreasing bank account, what you'll come back to on your return, what your friends and family might say and even the uncertainty of how you will spend your time. Will your career break experience live up to your expectations? And so much more.

We place many psychological, physical, and emotional barriers in our way to give us reasons not to take a career break, and if we allow them to take control, we will never achieve our dreams or have the experiences in life we feel passionate about.

As a career coach, an NLP practitioner, and an experienced career breaker, I wrote this book to:

1. help you determine whether a career break really is for you and why;
2. provide you with strategies to overcome the psychological barriers that may hold you back; and
3. help you get specific about where you want to go and what you want to do.

This book will also provide you with:

1. exercises to help keep you focussed, motivated, and committed to achieving your goals;
2. quotes, statistics, and information to assist you in making informed decisions along your journey; and
3. real-life examples from myself and others who have "made the break" and lived to tell the tale (emotionally, physically, and financially!).

Your Career Break: the *'how to'* guide is a career break *workbook*, which differentiates it from any other career break book. What also makes this book different is that it *doesn't* cover many of the practical aspects of taking a career break, such as renting your property, where to store your personal belongings, how to apply for visas, or what to pack if you choose to travel. If you're looking for this information, then head to the back of the book for some recommended websites and books.

Chapter 1:

WELCOME TO YOUR CAREER BREAK

Is This Book for You?

If you've ever found yourself dreaming of doing something different in your life that will take longer than your annual holiday allowance, then a career break may be right for you. Consider the following questions.

- Is there something you want to *achieve* that isn't being fulfilled by your work, relationships, or home life?
- Are you thinking about taking your life in a new *direction*?
- Do you want to *challenge* yourself and *step outside* your comfort zone?
- Are you looking for something more *meaningful* in life?
- Do you flip through magazines and wonder what it would be like to *experience* what you see in the pictures?
- Do you like the sound of doing something *different* with your life?
- Do you think about *contributing* to society?
- Are you looking for more *work–life balance*?

If any of these resonate with you, then it may be that you need a career break ... *now! So this book is definitely for you!*

In an ideal world you could just quit your job and start planning your break without a care in the world; however, you and I both know that unless you've won the lottery, you're going to have to put a little bit more thought and planning into extracting yourself from the clutches of society and everything in your life that ties you to where you are now. But that is all part of the process and a journey you have to take, so you might as well sit back and enjoy the ride.

If you're like me, or many of your friends, you've probably got property, furniture, pets, plants, debts, and a whole host of other possessions you've collected over the years. Not to mention a career, friends, family, and maybe a romantic relationship. You may be stuck in a rut, fed up, regretting never having had a chance to travel when you were young, thinking about changing jobs and needing a break in between, wanting to contribute to society and longing to do some volunteer work or perhaps to work abroad and gain some international experience, or you might just want to travel and see the world independently. Whatever your reason(s), this book will help motivate you to turn your career break dream into a reality.

Career Break Statistics

Did you know that more and more people today are taking career breaks? Around 90,000 people in the UK each year are taking a career break or a sabbatical, compared to 230,000 young people on a gap year (www.gapadvice.org/index.php/career-breaks). Gap Year for Grown Ups, the leading gap provider, has seen record growth in bookings - up 300 percent since 2005. Traditionally, gap years have been perceived to be the domain of school leavers, but the Gap Year for Grown Ups customer base now tells a different story; 61 percent are between twenty-five and fifty, 27 percent are over fifty, and only 12 percent are under twenty-five (www.gapyearforgrownups. co.uk).

According to research undertaken by Santander Credit Cards (4 September 2010), "Britain has seen a 14-fold rise in the number of people taking gap years, sabbaticals and other lifestyle breaks since the 1970s, including a remarkable spike since the recession began in 2008." The research reveals that the number of people taking time out from work and education has risen from 270,000 in the 1970s to four million between 2000 and 2010. Interestingly, 1.2 million of these lifestyle breaks have taken place since the recession began in

2008 (www.everyinvestor.co.uk/personal-finance/savings/recession-drives-spike-in-gap-years-and-sabbatical).

Santander go on to say that "just over one in ten (12%) UK adults has taken a lifestyle break in the past and a further four million (8%) Brits are currently planning one for the future" (www.everyinvestor.co.uk/personal-finance/savings/recession-drives-spike-in-gap-years-and-sabbatical).

Despite being common in many countries, such as Australia and the United Kingdom, career breaks, life sabbaticals, "gap years," and other forms of extended travel are not as common in America. It seems to be a common assumption that only a small number of Americans hold passports. Reasons vary as to why this is the case, and in his article "How Many Americans Have a Passport?" Matt Stabile notes that the cost of taking a family abroad may be one of the main reasons that Americans are reluctant to travel (http://www.theexpeditioner.com/2010/02/17/how-many-americans-have-a-passport-2/).

Wikipedia also notes that, given the size of America and how far international borders exist from most states, people tend not to travel abroad, which could be attributed to the lower number of passport holders in relation to the population. The number of passports issued in America peaked in 2007, with over 18 million; however, for the next three years numbers decreased, seeing just over 13 million issued (including 1.3 million passport cards) in 2012 (http://www.theexpeditioner.com/2010/02/17/how-many-americans-have-a-passport-2/). Some weight is also given to the theory that distance from national borders directly impacts on the numbers of passports held, as North Dakota, South Dakota, and Wyoming held the lowest number of passports issued, and California, New York, and Texas, all states close to international borders, held the highest number.

In the period 2008–2009, issued passports dropped by 2.7 million. No specific reason is stated for the decrease over the one-year period, though it may be fair to suggest that the global financial crisis and, as noted by Matt Stabile, stricter air travel requirements affected the number of American citizens making passport applications to travel abroad. It might be worth noting that the only other dip between the years 1974 and 2009 was during 1989–1992, which may be attributed to the economic recession, more specifically, the savings and loan crisis in America, which created the greatest banking collapse since the Great Depression in 1929 (www.useconomy.about.com/od/grossdomesticproduct/p/89_Bank_Crisis.htm) and jeopardised the financial well-being of millions of Americans (Wikipedia).

Whilst career breaks might not be an American birthright, the founders of Meet, Plan, Go! (www.meetplango.com) – Sherry Ott and Michaela Potter are on a mission to change that. For the past 3 years they have been speaking and writing about career breaks on their website. In addition they schedule events and meetups across America aimed at individuals contemplating a career break. Sherry Ott comments on her observations of the events: "People come to Meet Plan Go! events in order to be a part of a supportive travel community, and get inspiration and advice on how to do extended travel as mid-career adult. A career breaker is different than a gap year traveller. Career breakers often have more invested physically in their life; house, kids, pets, cars, aging parents, and a career. Therefore they have special concerns around how to put their life on hold and travel. In addition, by surrounding themselves by others who have experience or want to experience extended travel on their career break they are more likely to achieve their goals and stay motivated to work through the hard planning times".

Meet, Plan, Go! is passionate about encouraging those thinking about a career break to take the leap, give them the tools on how, and help them achieve their dreams! For more information on their events and resources, visit their website, www.meetplango.com.

As for Australia, 49 percent of the population hold passports (http://www.traveltrends.biz/ttn555-record-number-of-australians-hold-passport-to-adventure), which should be no surprise, given the reputation of Australians' love of travel. You may also find a Canadian sitting next to you on a plane, train, or automobile, as 70 percent of Canadians hold passports and also hold a reputation for travel and adventure (http://www.canada.com/Canadians+passports+early+next+year/2717953/story.html).

One of the fastest-growing countries issuing passports is India, with a reported annual growth of 20 percent in the last few years. Only 5 percent of India's 1.2 billion population currently hold passports (http://www.deccanchronicle.com/channels/nation/north/passport-three-days-new-project-roll-out-soon-971), and only 1.5% of the population of China hold a passport, though given their well-known work ethic and limited annual leave allowance, this figure comes as little surprise (http://french.china.org.cn/english/government/194422.htm).

The purpose of sharing all the passport statistics and information is to highlight the differences in cultures and countries regarding the number of passports issued. And, whilst the data may not be directly linked to career breaks, it certainly allows us to assume more and more people are travelling or spending time abroad.

Career Break Opinions

Why has the number of people taking career breaks and sabbaticals increased so dramatically over the years? It would be fair to firstly comment, as evidenced by Santander, that the recession has driven a spike in gap years and sabbaticals since 2008. Certainly, the opportunity to take a career break is more accessible with changing attitudes of employers, who now see the benefit of allowing employees to take sabbaticals, and the recognition and acknowledgment that those who return from a career break may have new skills and new qualifications and may come back with new-found enthusiasm for their job. Furthermore, once on a career break, the opportunities available to you are endless, especially with the wealth of volunteer organisations ready to assist you in experiencing your charitable dream. Furthermore, flights are cheaper and will take you just about anywhere in the world.

When I was growing up, who had the biggest house, the most expensive car, and the coolest swimming pool (I'm Australian, so a swimming pool was *very* important) was on the lips of every kid. The competition was ferocious, as you were judged by what you "owned," where you "lived," and what you "did." I'm confident these judgements still exist in most societies and cultures today; however, in more recent times "where you've travelled" has been added to the list. Conversations and stories are shared amongst friends, colleagues, and family about all the places they've been to or are planning to visit. Not to mention the plethora of websites to choose from where we can share our holiday photos with our friends and family. It's also surprising just how many people, as noted earlier, have taken career breaks, with some taking more than just one. As this number is on the increase, it raises the question, "Are our values changing?" Are we breaking free from society's expectations? Are we still allowing what we do, where we live, and what we own define us? Are we looking for more meaning in the world? More experiences? More fulfilment? More time for ourselves?

Debbie Norman, age fifty-five, from Kent, United Kingdom (UK), spent thirty-five years working in banking. After taking her first sabbatical, sailing on the Queen Mary 2 (a dream Debbie had held for many years) and travelling the west coast of America, she soon realized that even though she earned good money, enjoyed job security, and had enough disposable income to travel and buy whatever she wanted, her job wasn't fulfilling her needs. She soon became disengaged, disillusioned, and unhappy. A year later, Debbie realised there was more to life than working to live and subsequently changed her life by taking early retirement and setting up her own business selling vintage clothing.

It would be fair to say that over the years the nature of the job market has changed considerably with the introduction of various types of employment contracts, such as short-term contract work, temporary to permanent contracts, and interim and maternity cover assignments. Given the impermanency of these types of contracts, it makes it easier for people to take time off in between contracts to go travelling, undertake study, learn a new skill, or do some volunteer work.

Organisations have also responded to employee feedback in their need for increased "work–life balance" and implemented work–life balance policies and recruited consultants, such as Australian life balance specialist Emma Grey (www.worklifebliss.com.au). WorkLifeBliss offers workshops on workplace flexibility, webinar programs for working parents and managers and a 'Home Study Program' for people looking to rise above the modern challenge of 'having it all'.

Whilst it's great to have it all – such as investing in property, the stock market, and business ventures – the opportunity to take time out to do something different or see the world is very tempting, and, let's face it, we can always earn more money when we return to work. Nothing, in my opinion, can replace unique experiences, memories, a collection of great photos, and a handful of new friends. I don't know about you, but when I'm on my deathbed, I'm going to be reminiscing about all the places I've seen, things I've learnt, people I've met, and experiences I've had – not how many properties I owned or how many shares I bought and sold. As Debbie Norman has quoted to me many times over the years, "We'll be a long time looking at the lid," so why not make the most of your life now?

Ted Harrington, from North London, UK, made the most of his situation after being made redundant from his job in the construction industry. After Ted got over the initial shock, he took the opportunity to do something that neither his friends nor his family thought him capable of—he climbed Mt Kilimanjaro. Ted had never done anything like this in his life, and he surprised everyone, even himself, by what he achieved. His mind is now open to all sorts of possibilities, and he's contemplating trekking Machu Picchu in Peru. If Ted hadn't been made redundant, he would never have known what he was capable of achieving, and he now believes that there's no limit to what he can achieve.

Ted, like many others, was affected by the global financial crisis, which saw many people lose their jobs. According to the Office of National Statistics (UK), in the UK construction industry alone over 107,000 people were made redundant in 2009. Looking across all industries to include manufacturing, retail trade, financial services, transport, public administration, and professional scientific and technical activities, the number of people who were made redundant between 2008 and 2010 was over one million (www.statistics.gov. uk/pdfdir/lmsuk0810.pdf).

If you've found yourself in this situation, you don't have to perceive it as a huge disaster. As with Ted, and many others, you could see it as an opportunity to make some changes in your life and do what you've always wanted to do, which may include taking some time off to reflect on your next move, travelling, studying, or moving abroad.

If travelling is on your agenda, it's now easier than ever to seize that opportunity, as organisations are continually sprouting to help you select and manage your ideal trip, from the traditional High Street (UK) travel agent to on-line travel agents, from volunteer organisations running open days to provide information on their projects abroad, to TV travel shows which transport you to a destination and really give you a taste of what it would be like to visit or even live there. And, of course, there are also plenty of travel books, travel magazines, and books like this one, to help you prepare for your impending departure. So if you're contemplating going abroad on your career break, with all of the literature at your fingertips you've got every reason in the world to start packing.

If you've taken a break before, then you're already one step ahead; however, if this is your first time (virgin career breaker), and you're looking for some help and *guidance* on how to effectively take a career break and manage the transition from one of working to one of being prepared emotionally, physically, and financially to take time out and experience something new, then this book is for you.

Chapter 2:

WHAT'S A CAREER BREAK ALL ABOUT?

What Is a Career Break?

A career break is a period of time taken out of your normal routine to do something completely different, such as travel, do some volunteer work, gain a new skill or a professional qualification, renovate your house, or simply work on your tan. The Career Break Site adds "it's also a chance to do something new and exciting … a chance to get out there and see the world" (www.thecareerbreaksite.com).

In an interview with Jeff Jung, founder of Career Break Secrets, he stated that "the important thing to remember about taking a career break is that it is merely a break to focus on you and your personal passions. It's a time to put all the energy you've poured into your career and invest it in yourself. Also, if you've spent time building a career, then you have experience and accomplishments to fall back on when you re-enter. You are not a graduate out of college with no real-world experience. All those great accomplishments you have are still valuable when you return from your break."

In an article titled "A Career Break Is Not Career Death," published on 23 February 2011 (and which attracted some every interesting and controversial comments), Andrew Bath, general manager of Poolia (www.poolia.co.uk) Banking and Financial Services Recruitment Agency, states that "employers know that a person doesn't lose their knowledge when they take a break. In the current skills shortage this creates a fresh pool of talent which fills important gaps. Employers see the benefits of those who've taken career breaks in terms of new skills others may not have, especially when dealing with people and making decisions." Finally, Bath says that "it's worth remembering that a career break does not have to mean the end of a career" (www. news.efinancialcareers.co.uk/Blogs_ITEM/newsItemId-29410).

Why Do People Take Career Breaks?

You will read many stories throughout this book of people who have taken career breaks and who share their reasons for stepping out of their daily routines to do something they've always wanted to do. As you can see from the list below, there are many reasons why people take career breaks. Do any of these sound familiar? You may even want to circle the ones that resonate most and are driving you toward the decision to take a career break.

- You feel burnt out and fed up.
- You're stuck in a rut and need a change of pace/scenery/ circumstances.
- You're looking for some new and exciting experiences.
- You were made redundant and now have the time and money to try something different.
- You want to contribute to society or do some volunteer work.
- You can't stand your boss.
- You want to learn a new skill or undertake some study.
- You're sick of working long hours.
- You're not getting the "buzz" out of your job anymore.
- You're bored.
- You have experienced a personal tragedy and want to get away.
- You're looking for a new direction in life.
- Your partner is taking a career break, and you want to go with him or her.
- You want to have a baby.

- You want to switch off and free your mind from the burden of your job.
- You've identified a hidden talent that you want to pursue.
- An intimate relationship ended and you want to get away.
- Your children have left home, and you and your partner have time to do something together.
- It will make you happy.
- You want to feel that sense of freedom, with no boss telling you what to do.
- You need to care for a sick relative.
- You're seeking a new challenge.
- You've been lucky enough to come into some money, and it's burning a hole in your pocket.
- You want to retrain or upskill.
- It might just provide you with the changes in life you're looking for.
- You've hit the big 30, 40, 50, or 60.
- You're looking to change careers and want to take some time out to consider your options.
- You don't feel a connection to your company's values.
- You sit at your desk thinking, "There's got to be more to life than this."
- You want to spend some "quality time" with your family.
- You want to.
- You can.

Sherry Ott believes that "technology and culture have contributed to more people wanting and needing to take career breaks. As more and more people work longer hours at jobs that they are unable to 'unplug' from, we are finding that more people are reaching their burnout limit. In addition, the culture of how we look at our career has slowly been changing with each generation. On average people change jobs 5 times in their career, the loyalty to their employers is diminishing and the younger generation is starting to demand more time away or ability to work away from an office environment. These corporate cultural changes and technological changes are what is driving more and more interest in career break and travel. People are looking at career break travel as a way to unplug and break away to build their skills and knowledge, re-energize, and reconnect with their creativity. They come back to the workforce refreshed." (www.briefcasetobackpack.com).

During an interview with volunteer recruitment manager, Sophie Pell, Raleigh International, she stated that they "find that people choose to take a career break for one or more of the following reasons; learning new skills, taking time out to reflect and put perspective on where they are in their life, taking time to think about their career path and look at new options as well as wanting to do something worthwhile and meaningful."

Simone Schneider, from Germany, reflected on why she took a career break: "I was so involved in my daily routine that I didn't take the time to think about what I actually needed. I put all my energy into my work and my employer took it without any regret. As I was so involved in my work and the pressure, dependence and overtime that comes with it, I didn't see what it was doing to me. I was tired, weak and had lost all motivation. I knew then something had to change and for me it was taking a career break to find myself again."

Jon Stewart took his first career break at the age of twenty-five, after finding himself three years into a job that wasn't really going anywhere. He had fallen into a position as a temp after studying English at Leeds University (UK). Having left university in the middle of the recession in the mid-1990s, he managed to find a job in his hometown and so went back to living with his parents. Jon notes, "I was directionless, looking upwards in the company and seeing only the backsides of the people above me. I had absolutely no idea what different jobs were out there. Merchant banking. I don't want to work 24 hours a day. Marketing. I don't want to start by selling things from the back of a car." Jon was left thinking, "Perhaps I should have visited the university careers service more than once!"

Jon then went on a summer holiday with a friend, and whilst driving through the mountains of Italy was complaining about his lot in life when his friend suggested he join him in the south of Spain. Jon says the conversation went something like this:

Jon: I hate my job. I really don't know what I'm going to do. They want me to apply for a promotion in logistics, but I really don't know what that is, and I care even less.

Friend: Why don't you throw your job in, then? It sounds horrific! Come out to Spain. Do some teaching to earn some money and learn Spanish too. It will be good fun and you can stay with me until you sort things out.

Jon: But I don't have a teaching qualification.

Friend: It doesn't matter. You don't need that. You know English and it's not difficult to teach.

Five minutes later ...

Jon: Okay. Let's do it!

So, Jon returned from his holiday in Italy, enlivened and reborn. He resigned from his job, much to the surprise of his manager, and headed out to the beautiful, historic, and picturesque town of Granada to live and teach English.

Thirty-seven-year old Bal Mudhar from London, was stuck in a rut at work and desperate for something to change. After working for the same company for fifteen years Bal took voluntary redundancy. Even though Bal had moved around the organisation, taking on various roles and projects, what drove her to make the decision was the thought of working on one more project with the same people; she was experiencing a case of "same ol', same ol'." From the moment taking redundancy became an option, all Bal could do was think about what she could do with her time and money. She said that "the floodgates opened and suddenly all these opportunities started to appear." She realised she could do anything she wanted and had the financial means to do it. An exciting time lay ahead of her in both the planning and her actual career break. She says as soon as she started telling people about her plans, everyone was very supportive and started suggesting places for her to go and people with whom she could stay with across the globe.

Jon Palin took his second career break at the age of thirty-three after working as an actuary–financial consultant. Many reasons led Jon to take his twelve-month break, including:

- *Variety.* He'd spent his life studying and working with technical subjects, and his first career break had been to go back to university for a year, so he wanted to try something completely different.

- *Lack of stimulation at work.* He'd reached a senior position where work was becoming more routine, without the challenge of learning new things. He was also questioning the social value of what he did in the financial world.

- *Time of life.* He had the financial stability to take time off work and wanted to try something different before potentially settling down with a family, when it would be harder to make such a change.

- *Seeing others do it.* He thinks he would have been more apprehensive if he hadn't seen a few friends thrive after taking a different direction in life.

Jon feels his career break has changed him in many ways and says he now feels happier dealing with uncertainty; he is more prepared to go with the flow, rather than wanting everything to be planned out well in advance, and he's also realised there's more to life than a very structured job. Jon is now considering self-employment and reviewing how he can fit consulting and contracting around travel and more volunteering.

You may have noticed, from the individuals we've met so far, a few common themes threading through each story: dissatisfaction at work, time of life, and wanting to try something different. If you're concerned about taking some time out of your career, that's totally understandable, and you wouldn't be alone in your thinking. Jon Palin said he'd been pondering taking a career break for about a year before he decided to do it and says that making the decision was the biggest challenge, alongside deciding what do with his time when faced with a huge range of possibilities.

Tracey Baldwyn had also been thinking about a career break for years before finally taking the plunge at the age of forty-four. Even though some of her family members didn't understand her decision, she was resigned to the fact that she needed some time off from her demanding, all-absorbing, stressful job as a procurement manager in financial services, to re-evaluate her life and think about what she really wanted, plus have a well-deserved rest.

In chapter 3, "Getting Clear," you will be asked to complete an exercise that will help you define *why* you are thinking about making the break. So, whilst your brain is probably buzzing right now with the many reasons why you want a career break, I promise you will have an opportunity to articulate, very soon, your reasons and become very clear in your big *why*.

Is a Career Break Right For You?

Do you find yourself sitting at your desk dreaming of the day when you can get up when you want, not when the alarm trills in your ear; if there is something you want to achieve and you haven't yet found the time; if you have lost sight of what's really important in life; if you're looking for more meaning in the world; if you're fed up commuting with thousands of other people; if you just can't come to terms with the idea that you may have to work longer than you'd thought and by the time you retire you'll have grey hair, a pension pass, and a handful of grandchildren. If you relate to any of these, then a career break is definitely right for you.

It may be that you are thinking about taking a career break because you want to run away from a situation; you can't face being in familiar surroundings, and a change of scenery is what you need. If this is the case, ask yourself, "Is a career break what I need *right now?*" Or should you be staying at home and dealing with the situation at hand?

The one thing you've probably noticed that's missing from the list above is, "Do you have the *finances* to support a career break?" Whilst having the financial capacity to take a career break is important, you'll notice it's not the main focus of this book; it's simply one element in the big picture. You have the power to choose whether you make finances a deal breaker. If you wish to jump ahead and read more on this subject, skip to the section at the end of this chapter, "When should you take a career break?" where we'll discuss the financial situation. Furthermore, in chapter 5, in the section entitled "Paid Work" you can read about the various options if you choose to work during your career break.

It's pretty common for people to get bogged down with reasons why taking a career break *can't be done* and to say to themselves, "I can't take time out of my career," "I can't afford it," or "What about my mortgage and bills?" These are all fair reasons, and we'll examine these in chapter 4, "Making It Happen." But think about the reasons it *can be done* and how you'll feel if you allow yourself the time do something you've always wanted to do! Will you feel a sense of satisfaction? Will you feel free? Will you feel happy? Let your mind start creating all the possibilities.

Throughout this book, many contributors talk about how taking a career break has given them a different perspective on life and on some occasions has led them to make significant changes, such as embarking on a new career, establishing more work–life balance or changing the way they approach life. Consider Jeff Jung, the aforementioned founder of Career Break Secrets, who held a successful career as a medical-device marketing director and management consultant. He made a decision that would change his life forever. Jeff, like many others, felt that whilst he enjoyed a successful life with a good job, a beautiful home, close friends, and family, he didn't have control over his life. Work–life balance became just words, and everything he enjoyed in life took a backseat to the work that dictated much of his life. When Jeff made the decision to step out of his professional life, his friends called him brave – and also crazy – but he says he'll never regret the decision and is determined to prove that you can have a successful career without letting it run your life. Jeff shares the full details of his story in his article "The Sabbatical: Personal Revival" in *Case in Point,* the official magazine of the Case Management Society of America (http://careerbreaksecrets.com/about-us/jeff-jung-founder).

If you can relate to Jeff's story, or maybe even know someone who's taken a career break, then it's time to consider these questions:

- How can I make it happen?
- Whom do I need to speak to?
- How will I decide what to do and where to go?
- How much money will I need?
- What characteristics, traits, and qualities do I need to sustain my decision?
- Who will support me?
- How will I deal with possible resistance from my family and friends?
- How will I keep myself on track to ensure I have the financial capacity to do what I want?

Using the space below, list any other questions you might need to consider.

_____

_____

_____

_____

_____

Throughout the book, you'll undertake a host of exercises to help you address all of the questions above, and perhaps you've identified some yourself, to help you achieve your goal of taking the career break you've been dreaming about.

Career Break or Sabbatical?

You may have also heard the term *sabbatical*. So what's the difference between a career break and a sabbatical? These words are sometimes used interchangeably; however, according to Gap Year for Grown Ups, "a sabbatical is a system whereby companies allow their employees to take an extended period of leave above their usual holiday allowance—with the guarantee that their job will held open for them when they return" (www.gapyearforgrownups.co.uk/ Sabbatical). Employees may have to qualify to take a sabbatical, and each company will have a different policy with specific criteria. For a comprehensive list of companies across North America and Europe offering sabbaticals, visit the Workplaces for Sabbaticals page at yoursabbatical.com. Furthermore, they also provide facts and figures on sabbatical movements, sabbaticals in recession, and details on sabbatical trends.

Debbie Norman took a six-month sabbatical from her job in banking. As Debbie had been working for the bank for over ten years, she qualified to apply. As Debbie's company operated a formal sabbatical policy, her job was held open, so that she slid straight back in on her return. Ann Sullivan, from Gloucester, UK, took a three-month sabbatical from her job in an insurance company and travelled through South East Asia. On her return to England, she returned to her role working in human resources.

Corbett Barr, corporate escapee turned entrepreneur, freelancer and blogger, based in San Francisco, became self-employed in 2006. In his blog, Free Pursuits, he wrote an article entitled "10 Lessons Learned on a 6-Month Sabbatical" after returning from his sabbatical travelling through Mexico. Corbett states, "The rumours have not been exaggerated. Taking a sabbatical is an amazing, rejuvenating, life-changing experience. Spending time in a new place or country away from the daily grind can help you see life in a completely new way" (www.freepursuits.com/10-lessons-learned-on-a-6-month-sabbatical).

Employers' Opinions

Interestingly, over the last few years, employers' attitudes have changed as they're realising that to retain good employees, they may have to release them for a certain period of time. It may well be in the organisation's best interests to encourage sabbaticals, especially during uncertain economic times; however, the organisation may also benefit from an employee who returns with new skills, maybe a new language or a professional qualification, in addition to a renewed and refreshed attitude towards work.

Gapadvice.org report that many companies now have an "enlightened view of career breaks, an extension of the sabbaticals which many people teaching overseas receive. They realise that breaks allow staff to acquire new skills and that it is better to retain quality, motivated staff than to keep unhappy staff whose heart is not in the job" (http://www.gapadvice.org/index.php/career-breaks).

Offering sabbaticals may also help reduce the cost of recruitment and increase retention. The cost of keeping key employees happy by allowing them to take a sabbatical is more effective than watching them leave, taking with them all the institutional knowledge they've developed over the years, the investment in their training and development, and possibly their contacts and clients, not to mention the disruption to the team (www.fierceinc.com/index.php?page=blog).

Coming from a background in recruitment, in my experience, costs incurred to replace employees can be expensive what with the high recruitment fees when utilising external consultants. Not to mention the amount of time it takes to source and screen candidates, undertake interviews (of which there can be many), deliberate each candidate with key hiring managers, make an offer to the successful candidate, provide feedback to unsuccessful candidates, create contracts, negotiate compensation and benefits, and depending on the level of the candidate, the company may have to wait up to three months before the new recruit commences. And, once they join it can take months for them to get up to speed. Taking everything into consideration, it appears that the cost of replacing good workers far outweighs the cost of providing a sabbatical and keeping them happy. Who wouldn't want to work for an "employer of choice" who provides a sabbatical policy where employees are able to spend time away from the office to do something they've always wanted to do, secure in the knowledge they have a role to come back to? It's a win-win!

"Yomps" adventure travel experience also discuss how career breaks and sabbaticals are advantageous for employees and companies alike, in that during uncertain economic times companies have recognised that by giving employees time off they are "giving extra life to the employees and getting an extra few years of service from them, thus not losing their skills and getting new skills from their employees on their return to work" (www.yomps.co.uk/travel-resources/articles/15462/how-to-ask-your-company-for-a-career-break).

Yomps share some useful tips in their article "How to Ask Your Company for a Career Break." These tips include the following:

1. Be clear about what you want to do during your career break.
2. Speak to your manager or HR, explain how long you've been working in the company and what you want to do on your career break.
3. Listen carefully and pick up any information that will help you with your application.
4. Write a good letter addressing any concerns the company may have, discuss what you want to do, and promote the positives.
5. Submit your application and cross your fingers.

Yomps say that companies are more likely to approve your career break or sabbatical if you are taking time out to learn a new skill, undertake volunteer work, or gain skills that will help the company in the long run (www.yomps.co.uk/travel-resources/articles/15462/how-to-ask-your-company-for-a-career-break).

Depending on your approach and your company, you may wish to follow the simple steps suggested by Yomps. However, for a more detailed approach, here are a few more steps:

Step 1: Find out whether your company offers a sabbatical policy and, if so, what are the minimum and maximum lengths of time offered. Are there any forms you have to fill out? Whom would you need to inform? What perks and benefits, such as pension/superannuation, health insurance, would be suspended for the duration? What perks or benefits would be continued?

Step 2: Be prepared. Before meeting your manager, arm yourself with information on when you want to take your break, how long you want to be away for, what you plan to do, and how your workload could be managed whilst you're away. Make it easy on your manager, and do the thinking for him or her.

Step 3: Set up a meeting with your manager to discuss your sabbatical. Think about the questions you may be asked, write them down, and have the answers ready. It may be that you'll have to negotiate the timing of your break due to the nature of your role or the industry you work in. There may be a more "natural" time to step away from the organisation, causing minimal disruption to you and your team. Share with your manager the benefits of your taking a break and how this could impact the organisation in a positive way. If there is someone in your team looking to take on more responsibility or make a change in their role, then highlight this to your manager as this may provide a good learning and development opportunity for this colleague, which in turn, may retain the colleague, in the event they were seeking a new challenge elsewhere.

Step 4: Once your sabbatical is agreed upon, complete the necessary paperwork and return it to the appropriate parties. Ensure you have all the dates confirmed and agreement on which perks and benefits are suspended and which continued.

Step 5: Organise your farewell party!

Despite all your careful planning and preparation, your manager may still reject your application, or your company may not offer a sabbatical policy. If so, what are your options? First and foremost, you can decide to put your career break plans on hold and try again at a later date. Or, depending on your attitude to risk, you always have the option to resign from your job. Making the decision to resign from your job can be quite exciting and exhilarating for some, but stressful for others; it is often what holds people back from taking a career break. Later, in chapter 4, we discuss mind over matter and limiting beliefs, and provide you with exercises to help you overcome obstacles such as fear, to help give you the confidence to make the decision to turn your break into a reality.

If you're sitting on the fence as to whether you would consider resigning from your job, what may help you is writing a pros and cons list to help you in your decision making. Here are a few to get you started.

Pros to resigning

- You will have total freedom to do what you want, when you want.
- Your break is unlimited, allowing you the opportunity to take off as long as you like.
- It's a clean break and provides an opportunity to start fresh on your return.
- It could be an escape from a job or boss you don't like.
- It's an opportunity to try a different job on your return and meet new people.
- You may find a job, on your return, that pays more than your last one (it happens!).
- On your return, you may find a more rewarding and challenging job.

Cons to resigning

- You would lack job security on your return.
- You would lose your company benefits (if you have any benefits).
- You may face some market challenges when job hunting on your return.

In the space below, record your own pros and cons.

Pros

_____

_____

_____

Cons

_____

_____

_____

Depending on your personal circumstances, and your attitude to risk, resigning from your job may or may not cause a problem for you. Doug Kington spent many years working in the retail sector in London. The companies he worked for didn't offer sabbatical policies, so every time he took a career break, he had to resign. Doug was pretty laid-back about this, as he was quite confident on his return to London he would find a job quite quickly and easily. However, in 2009, after returning from one of his career breaks, Doug struggled to source a job back in retail and found himself working for a few months in a job he disliked. It didn't take Doug long to realise he wanted another break, so off he went. Considering Doug didn't like his job, this made the decision easier.

Ann Sullivan utilised her company's sabbatical policy and returned to her role after her first career break. However, on her return from her second career break, Ann had to start her job search again, as she had taken voluntary redundancy from her previous role. Ann decided to take on a domestic role when she returned, to give her the time and space to consider her next move. It was only six weeks later that Ann found a position back in human resources, working for a different company.

From a personal perspective, one month after returning from my first career break back in 2006, I secured a job that paid me over £15,000 more than the job I had left. What a sweet deal! After my second career break, the market was a different story. Even with over ten years of recruitment, training, and development experience, I found it a challenge to get a job. Companies wanted me to jump through hoops, and on one occasion I had eleven interviews and was eventually told the company had initiated a recruitment freeze (very frustrating).

Some of my friends who work in the same field and had also taken career breaks shared similar stories about how, after returning from their career breaks, they spent three months looking for a job and attended a plethora of interviews before securing a role.

On the positive side, though, I ended up in a role that was perfect for me and paid me more than the job I left before my eighteen-month career break. I am a big believer in fate and that you end up exactly where you're supposed to. I know in my heart that I was meant to be working where I was at the time of writing this book.

In summary, if a sabbatical is not available to you, then the following steps are all you need to embark on your career break if you decide to resign.

Step 1: Decide what you want to do (stay at home, go abroad, volunteer) and where you want to go.

Step 2: Resign from your job.

Step 3: Organise your farewell party!

Finally, it pays to be organised, regardless of whether you're taking a sabbatical or a career break. If you are taking a sabbatical, clearly there are more steps involved and possibly a series of approvals lie ahead. The key is being prepared and arming yourself with all the information so that the only option for your employer is to say *yes!*

If you want to assist and encourage your organisation to develop their career break policy, direct them to your.sabbatical.com (www.yoursabbatical.com), which helps businesses create and implement sabbatical programmes designed to attract, retain, and accelerate top talent through personal and professional enrichment. Their starting premise is that talented people entering the workforce consistently rate "time off" as a top priority (money comes third) and that "sabbaticals designed properly result in enormous returns for individual sabbatical-goers, their work coverage teams and their companies' performance."

How to Sell your Career Break

According to Charlotte Hindle (pg 2-3) "a future employer will judge whether your career break was a positive step or not by how you choose to spend your time. Some activities will enhance your CV such as learning a new skill (such as a language), working as a volunteer, achieving personal goals (e.g. sailing around the world), or gaining experiences valuable to your current or future profession".

For those who resigned from their job to take a break, the way you present your career break to prospective employers could make or break a job offer. Here are some tips:

1. Present your career break positively and talk about it constructively during an interview

2. Share your new found enthusiasm for returning to work and how your career break has revitalized you and you're now ready to 'get back into it'

3. Stress what you learned, what you achieved and what value this will add to your future employer. These might include:

- Teamwork and collaboration
- Adapting to different cultures and customs
- Communication skills
- Commitment and dedication
- Working in adverse conditions
- Overcoming obstacles and problem solving
- Teaching others
- Delegating
- Responsibility
- Project management
- Planning and implementation
- Managing budgets
- Adaptability and flexibility
- Change orientated
- Resilience
- Proactivity
- Willingness to take on a new challenge

Your CV

Always account for the time you spent on your career break or sabbatical on your CV. Prospective employers will notice gaps in your CV and if time is unaccounted for and it could lead to assumptions and judgements on *how* and *where* you spent your time. So, take out the ambiguity and be open about what you achieved.

At the end of your CV, create the title '*Career Break or Sabbatical*' and state the month and year you took your breaks (be specific) and state what you did in that time. You don't have to list everything but provide a few key points as per the example below. Employers will be able to see what you accomplished during your break and may wish to discuss your experiences during your interview.

Career Breaks

Study and travel

- February 2009 – October 2010 (*Study* – Certificate in Life Coaching. *Travel* – Australia, Vietnam, Thailand, Laos, Cambodia)
- October 2005 – April 2006 (USA, Australia, Thailand, Hong Kong & volunteering in Taiwan)

Selling your career break during your interview

If you resigned from your job prior to your career break you will go through the process of looking for a job ether before you return or once you've arrived home. It's imperative that you are prepared to discuss and account for your career break as prospective employers will be interested to hear about your experiences.

During an interview, your interviewer(s) may ask you questions surrounding the competencies required to perform the role, such as teamwork, budget and project management, managing others or problem solving. They will be looking for you to provide examples of where you have exhibited these behaviours and competencies. This presents an opportunity for you to sell the skills you may have acquired on your career break when formulating your answers.

To prepare yourself for an interview, write down any possible questions you may be asked focusing on the competencies and duties of the role then consider how you would go about responding. For example:

Question 1: Tell me about a time where you had to manage a project from start to finish.

- What was the project?
- Who was involved?
- How did you allocate roles to the team?
- Were there any problems?
- How did you overcome them?

- What was the result?
- What would you have done differently?

Question 2: How would you describe your management style?

- When was the last time you managed a team?
- How many people did you manage?
- What would your team say about you?
- How would your manager describe your style?
- What is it about your style that differentiates you from others?
- What do you like the most about managing others?
- What do you like the least about managing others?

Question 3: Describe a problem that you recently encountered and how you overcame it?

- What was the problem?
- How did you identify the problem?
- Who did you involve to help you?
- What did you do to overcome the problem?
- What future strategies did you put in place to avoid the problem occurring again?
- What did you learn from this?

By writing down the possible questions and answers you will be more prepared and able to describe your experiences in a more articulate, concise and professional manner. In the many years I worked in recruitment, I always found it more interesting if a candidate used a variety of examples when answering questions. I'm not suggesting you restrict your answers to your career break experiences, but include a few to keep the interviewers interested. If you are unsure about which example to use, just ask the interviewer, for example:

Interviewer: Tell me about a time you had to create and manage budgets?

You: In fact, I have a couple of examples I can use, such as when I managed the finance department's budget in my last job as an accountant or when I was a Project Manager on a volunteer project in Costa Rica and managed the budget for the region. Which would you prefer?

Using this strategy gives the interviewer an opportunity to choose which example they would like to hear. Plus, it shows you have expansive experience in this area and are able to draw examples from a variety of sources.

Let's use one example and go through the entire question and answer process.

Question 1: Tell me about a time where you had to manage a project from start to finish.

What was the project?	I spent 3 months volunteering in India and was tasked with project managing the building of a small school for the local children. The children currently have to walk 4 miles to the nearest school, so by building one in the local village this will provide a safer environment for the children and they won't have to walk as far. Furthermore, the parents can keep a closer eye on them.
Who was involved?	About 8 other volunteers, a handful of local workers and the supplier of all the building materials.
How did you allocate roles to the team?	I paired up a volunteer with a local worker as I thought this would benefit both parties in that they got to work closely with someone from another culture, teach each other their language and customs, plus the local person could talk with the suppliers and perhaps interpret when required, with the intention of speeding up processes.

Were there any problems?	The main problems centred around communication and the availability and delivery of the building materials. The materials didn't always turn up on time, so it affected the time-scale and completion date of the project. We also experienced a few days where it rained consistently so this put our project on hold until such time we could continue the build.
How did you overcome them?	I requested more local volunteers to work on the project so we could catch up on the time lost and also altered the project plan. I also worked more closely with the local suppliers to try and understand the problems they faced and offered suggestions and advice as to how they could overcome them. Of course, this was taking into consideration the local customs and culture, to avoid causing any offence.
What was the result?	Whilst we had our fair share of challenges, which had to be addressed on a daily basis, the school was successfully built. We did run over time by one week, but considering the problems we experienced I thought that was a pretty good outcome.
What would you have done differently?	Probably make a more 'realistic' project plan and take into account the weather, the fact that things were 'done differently' there and completed a more thorough risk assessment. And ideally I would have allocated more local workers to the project.

From this example, the interviewer may / would have extracted the following competencies, skills and traits:

- Teamwork and collaboration
- Your management style

- Risk assessment skills
- Ability to adapt
- Flexibility in your approach
- Respect for others
- Understanding and adapting to other cultures and customs
- Analytical thinking

It may also help to 'role-play' a mock interview with a friend, or your coach, to test out your interview examples in an environment where you can make mistakes without any serious consequences. This way you'll be more prepared, confident and comfortable when you're sitting in front of a prospective employer and selling your career break experiences.

In summary, preparation is the key to successfully re-entering the work place on your return. Be open and honest about your experiences by stating it clearly on your CV and, if appropriate, utilise experiences from your career break when answering questions during your interview. Do your homework and any fears of securing a role will disappear very quickly.

Career Break Ideas

According to research conducted in 2010 by Santander Credit Cards, a massive 47 percent of people surveyed claimed that the opportunity to travel was their main reason for taking time out. However, some people simply wanted a rest (20%), the chance to work abroad (18%), or time for education and training (13%) (www.everyinvestor.co.uk/personal-finance/savings/recession-drives-spike-in-gap-years-and-sabbatical).

How will you spend your time?

- Travel—experience new cultures, customs, religions, food, and languages and meet the local people.

- Volunteer work—give back to society and do something meaningful, such as conservation work, work with animals, building homes and schools, or spending time in an orphanage.

- Learn a new skill—become a ski instructor, improve your cooking skills, or take acting classes.

- Move abroad and work full- or part-time whilst immersing yourself in a new culture.

- Gain a professional qualification—add something extra to your CV, and get that promotion.

- Learn a new language like Italian, French, or Arabic and impress your friends!

- Stay at home and relax, evaluate your career, renovate your house, or do those DIY jobs that never seem to get done.

- Undertake a degree—this may lead you to a new and exciting career.

- Write that book you've always wanted to. There may be a "Mills and Boon" author in you yet!

Why choose just one? During my first career break, I travelled, visited family and friends in Australia, and then spent a month volunteering in a children's home in Taiwan. Alison Light, from London, spent her career break at home. She learnt how to make the perfect scone and started a garden design course. Ted Harrington climbed Mt. Kilimanjaro and, after returning to the UK, did some volunteer work for a local charity.

Combine a few activities and really make your career break something to remember.

When to Take Your Career Break?

Is there a perfect time to take a career break? In short, no! Taking a career break is a personal decision and can be based on many things, such as your financial situation, the time of year, your career, or your family and other relationships. It may be that your career break has been forced upon you in the form of redundancy or pregnancy, so the decision as to when to take a career break was taken out of your hands.

Let's look at these in more detail.

Financial situation

It can be a bit of a challenge to take a career break if you don't have the financial capacity to support it, but it's not impossible. Your financial situation may impact the length of your career break and, if you're planning to go abroad, where you go and what you do. It may be fair to suggest that a healthy bank account will not only allow you to do what you want but will ease the pain of paying the bills if you have a mortgage, credit card debts, or other financial commitments whilst you're not working.

The results of research by Santander Credit Cards predict that, despite their increasing popularity, the *duration* of career breaks will reduce considerably, due to financial constraints, with 23 percent expecting to take three months or less, and 66 percent expecting to take less than twelve months (www.everyinvestor.co.uk/personal-finance/savings/recession-drives-spike-in-gap-years-and-sabbatical). So, if you want to spend more time away from work, ensure you are fully aware of your financial situation so that you don't find yourself having to return to work earlier than anticipated or, if you plan on travelling, on a plane heading back home having missed out on a host of experiences you didn't achieve because you couldn't afford them!

It is possible to take a career break with minimal funds, especially if you plan to work to support yourself during your break. For information on paid work during your career break, head to chapter 5, where you can read about possible options and hear from other career breakers who've worked to fund their experiences, like Mike Schimanowsky and Kelly Hale from Canada, Phil and Tammy Angel from Cairns, Australia and Kelly Taylor from London.

Even if you do plan to work, you may feel more comfortable reviewing your budget and detailing where you want to go and what you want to do (addressed in chapter 5) before you go, in order to avoid disappointment. It's always better to be prepared, and here are a few online resources to get you started.

- **careerbreakcafe.com** offers a Career Break Cash Flow Planner, where you can plan and track your budget (www.careerbreakcafe.com/career-break-money)

- **gapadvice.org** provides a Gap Cost Calculator to help you look carefully at the costs of your impending break (www.gapadvice.org/career-breaks/finance)

- **i-to-i Volunteer and Adventure Travel** offers suggestions on how to cure the financial headache of going on a career break and how to manage your money while you're away (www.i-to-i.com/how-to-manage-your-money)

The thought of budgets can send some of us running in the opposite direction, though budgeting doesn't have to be a daunting experience. If you're looking for some simple and easy budgeting steps that won't cause you too much pain, Leo Babauta, in his article "Simple Budgeting for Lazy People" (I'm not suggesting you're lazy; it's just the title of the article!), offers a few simple strategies to help you get started (www.zenhabits.net/cash). Whilst these are not specifically related to saving for a career break, they may provide you with some general ideas and guidance.

- Make a few lists—simply record your income and expenses, this way you can see how much is coming in and how much is going out.

- Simplify—live more simply by reducing your expenditures and eliminating the "nice to haves," such as magazine subscriptions, eating out, and new clothes.

- Make savings and debt payments first—make these mandatory every payday, even if the amount is minimal. They will add up over time.

- Make mandatory payments next—pay your bills automatically after every payday.

- What's left over is spending cash—this is for your groceries, petrol, entertainment, and saving for your career break.
- Long-term moves—over time you may want to eliminate all debt and free up your money for savings.

If you're still procrastinating about creating your budget, Leo's final piece of advice is, "You just need to sit down and do it, and not put it off" (www.zenhabits.net/cash). It isn't as scary as you have probably made out in your head. Simply create a spreadsheet and record your income and expenditures, take one away from the other, and what's left over save for your career break!

In her article "Can I Afford a Sabbatical?," posted 25 May 2011, Kimberly Palmer interviewed five people who managed to take sabbaticals from their full-time jobs and recorded their top ten tips, including managing finances. Read more from the individuals who contributed to the article, and see what strikes a chord with you, in particular the stories and examples on the following topics.

- Do whatever it takes to establish a healthy slush fund.
- Get your finances ultra-organised.
- Pay off lingering debts.
- Bring in extra cash.
- Don't wait until you can afford it.

(http://money.usnews.com/money/personal-finance/articles/2011/05/25/can-i-afford-to-take-a-sabbatical).

Bal Mudhar used the money she received from her voluntary redundancy package to support her career break and pay her mortgage and bills whilst she was away. As she didn't return to work immediately on her return, the remaining money was used to pay for her normal living expenses. Similar to Bal, Ted Harrington used his redundancy money to support his break. Whilst he used some of this to fund a couple of trips away, the remainder was used to pay for his day-to-day living expenses and other financial commitments until he found a job and returned to the workforce.

As you will read in my own "big *why*," I saved for two years to take my second career break, as I wanted to have the financial freedom and flexibility to do what I wanted, when I wanted, plus ensure that if anything unexpected cropped up, I had the finances to deal with it. I had a general idea of how much money I wanted and worked towards saving that amount. As far as budgeting, as soon as I got paid each month, I transferred a set amount of money into my online savings account and watched it steadily grow over time (which was very exciting), until such time I was happy with the amount and felt comfortable enough to make the break. As I didn't know how long my break was going to be, I ensured I had a very healthy bank account; I managed to save in excess of £30,000. Some may say I'm a little crazy saving (and spending) that much money on a career break, as it could be used as a deposit on a property. However, if I were to do it all over again, my decision would be the same. I often reflect on how my life would be different if I hadn't taken my career breaks and I'm sure I would not be in the privileged position of living and working in New York on an international assignment with my company.

The approach you decide to take will be a very personal one, as everyone has his or her own individual style to saving money. You may choose to ask a friend or family member to save your money on your behalf so that you won't be tempted to touch it, or, like me, you might set up a funds transfer every month, or maybe you will use your annual bonus (if you get one) and save in one big chunk. Whatever you decide, go for what works for you.

An important message to take away from this section is that whilst saving is imperative to your sabbatical or career break, it's also about changing your lifestyle in order for you to achieve your goals. You may decide to stay at home and cook dinner as opposed to going out, limit the new clothes you buy, reduce the amount of alcohol you drink, decrease your weekend getaways or expensive holidays, or cancel your gym membership and subscriptions to magazines and other publications. If you decide to take a sabbatical or career break with your partner, you may decide to live off one salary and save the other, which may help you achieve your goals faster. I'm sure there are some areas of your life where you would be able to limit your expenditures. Using the space below, list some of your initial ideas.

Areas where you can limit your expenditures:

_____

_____

_____

_____

_____

_____

_____

_____

The time of year

If you choose to stay at home during your break, there may be no "best" time of the year to do this, unless you have a specific project in mind, such as renovating your house, which may be better to do in the summer months. If you choose to travel at the most "popular" times of the year, be prepared to experience extra crowds, the possibility of hotels and backpacker hostels being fully booked or having limited availability, and, of course, the extra expense of travelling in peak season. However, travelling at these times may give you better weather conditions, more access to the events and festivals you'd like to attend, and the opportunity to meet lots of other travellers, like yourself.

During my second career break, a friend and I took a day trip from Phi Phi Island (Southern Thailand) that stopped off at Maya Beach (where they filmed the movie *The Beach,* starring Leonardo di Caprio). The postcards of Maya Beach depicted a deserted beach with crystal blue seas and the typical rock formations famous in Southern Thailand in the distance. A picturesque scene of tranquillity ... until we arrived and found ourselves sharing this scene with about two thousand other tourists wishing to experience the same view and feeling of serenity. Oh well, that's what you get for travelling in peak season!

The benefits of travelling off-season may include cheaper flights, fewer travellers, more available accommodation, easier access to locals, and less queuing. However, on the flip side, the climatic conditions may not suit your needs and events, and activities you wish to attend may run only at the peak times.

Climate

The weather may not be much of a concern for you; however, it could be vital to some events, such as skiing, sun baking, or surfing. Before booking your trip, ask your local travel agent or search the internet to review the yearly climatic conditions, which may impact your decision on where you go and what you do. You don't want to turn up in Asia only to be welcomed by the monsoon season. Or maybe you do, but it's best to be prepared and have all the information to hand before you go.

Even though I'm Australian, you'd think I would be used to the heat when visiting my family back in Brisbane. Alas, no! Queensland gets exceptionally hot and humid, and there is nothing worse than feeling sticky and sweaty all day. Besides, it's difficult to sleep unless your room has air-conditioning. A few years ago I headed to Egypt, where our tour group experienced forty-five-degree Celsius heat. The group found it quite challenging to actively listen to our tour guide inform us about the ancient Egyptians, as all we wanted to do was get out of the heat, get back on the bus, and into the pool.

Source: www.careerbreakcafe.com; Sue Hadden

Festivals and events

Certain events across the globe may occur only once a year, so if you're looking to attend the Rio Carnival in Rio de Janeiro, for example, then you'll need to visit in March. Just be aware that over 500,000 visitors attend the carnival, so booking in advance is highly recommended. A perfect place to start your search is at www.whatsonwhen.com, the worldwide events guide from Frommer's. This website provides information on a range of activities happening across the globe, covering areas such as arts, music and nightlife, sport and outdoors, lifestyle, kids and family, the weird and wonderful, festivals, and heritage.

List below any events you would like to experience.

_____

_____

_____

_____

_____

Your career

When negotiating a sabbatical or thinking about resigning from your job to take a career break, there are a few things to consider regarding your career.

1) Job market/economic conditions

With the recent economic climate and the global financial crisis, the job market has been extremely volatile. As noted earlier, the Office of National Statistics (UK) reported over one million people being made redundant between 2008 and 2010. During these times it may be a great opportunity to take some time off to avoid the environment, though you need to consider whether the industry you work in will be recruiting when you return.

2) The best time to leave and return

This may vary depending on the sector in which you work and if there are any natural cycles, though during certain times of the year it's much more of a challenge to secure a job, for example, Christmas, Easter, and the summer months. This is due to people being away on holidays or offices closing down for religious festivities.

Furthermore, if you stayed until the end of the year or financial year, would you be in a position to receive a bonus? If so, would that extra cash allow you to be away for longer or achieve more during your break?

3) Portability of your skills

Consider taking your skills on the road. Of course, this depends on what you do and if it's possible to work from any location in the world. If your work includes using the internet for jobs such as web design, writing, editing, and so on, then it's possible to become a freelancer, like Mike Schimanowsky and Kelly Hale from Canada, who packed up their worldly belongings, bade farewell to their friends and family, and traded in their nine-to-five jobs for a life of nomadic freelancing and travel. You can read more of their story in chapter 5. Similarly, Ann Sullivan completed a Teaching English as a Foreign Language (TEFL) course in the United Kingdom before moving to Bangkok to teach English to high school students.

Your family and relationships

Are you considering your family in your decision to take a break? Are you thinking of taking your family? Do you have a partner to take into account? Or are you going it alone? There are no rules or guidelines to help you make this decision, and your personal circumstances will dictate your choices.

The majority of career breakers I've met during my own travels have been single. It certainly makes life a bit easier if you have no one at home to consider; however, taking a break with your partner could be a wonderful experience to share. For example, friends of mine, Phil and Tammy Angel, moved from Australia to Wales many years ago. After saving for a few months, they jetted to Italy and spent six months working for a travel company, managing bike tours across Umbria and Tuscany. They returned to Wales but soon left for France to work the ski season purely for fun and the experience. I'm pleased to say they are now happily married and running a business together in Cairns, Australia. So it's fair to say that taking career breaks with your partner can be a success!

Taking your family on a career break has also attracted a lot of attention. An article in the *Sunday Times* (22 August 2010) entitled, "You're Never Too Young For a Gap Year," described the tales of a few families who have taken their children away on a gap year to either live abroad or travel. Whilst there are concerns regarding taking children out of the schooling system, there are counterarguments that other life experiences, such as getting to know different currencies, working out different values, and volunteering in orphanages, are of equal benefit and give children a broader view of the world.

The article also reported that British actress Emma Thompson thinks taking your child on a "baby gap year" is a good idea and that she intends to take her ten-year-old daughter, Gaia, on a year out. In fact, the topic has become so popular that the UK's Channel 4 aired a six-part series called *My Crazy Family Gap Year*.

Taking their kids on the road with them was a dream come true for the Meitler family of Newbury Park, California. The article "Family's School on Wheels Visits 30 States" talks about their experiences of travelling across America. Carole, Paul, and their four daughters, Katelyn, Rebecca, Christina, and Rachel, spent seven months in an RV, visiting Mount Rushmore, Niagara Falls, Gettysburg, Washington, national parks, and other historical sites. The children were already home-schooled, so taking them on the road was no different, other than that they would be experiencing history firsthand. Even the kids state that "it's the best education they've ever had," whilst Carole says "she would do it again in a heart-beat." (http://abclocal.go.com/kabc/story?section=news/local/ventura_county&id=6594362).

Single parent Karrie, in her blog RV Homeschool (www.homeschoolblogger.com/rvhomeschool), shares her inspiring plan to home school her two children whilst travelling across America and Canada. Karrie talks about all the aspects she had to consider when preparing for the trip, such as planning the routes, figuring out a solid budget, and sourcing on-line freelancing opportunities to supplement her income. Once Karrie had made the decision to take time out, she asked lots of questions and talked to friends and found a host of networks and people to support her in her endeavours. She was also surprised, but comforted, by how many other families were doing something similar.

As excited as Karrie was about her impending trip, she still worried about the kids getting sick, the trailer breaking down, and her concerns over hating the experience. There are never any guarantees that things are going to work out exactly as you'd like them to, and at the end of the day, that's life and you deal with whatever comes your way. Karrie identified quickly that she was talking herself down and knew that she would be able to deal with any crisis that prevailed. Whilst Karrie originally asked herself *how* she was going to achieve her dream, what kept her focused was her big *why!*

Redundancy

If you have been made redundant, then you may have little control over when you leave your job. However, you do have control over what you do next. For example, if you choose to head overseas or take some time out at home, you have the decision-making power to choose when to go and where you go, or how you spend your time at home.

A friend and co-worker took *voluntary* redundancy and a severance package back in 2006 from his HR role in a financial services organisation, due to lack of career opportunity. Some may say this gave him more control, as it was *his* decision to move on from the organisation and accept the terms of the package and the timing of his exit. Accepting these terms allowed him, at the age of forty, to spend more time with his family, improve his golf handicap, work out whether he could play internet poker, and try new things, such as cooking and painting. Whilst he missed the social side of work and the intellectual challenge, he enjoyed not having to shave every day or commute to work or have a nine-to-five day forced upon him.

Maternity leave

This one may also be out of your control, so when to take your maternity career break could be unpredictable and unplanned. Tracey Baldwyn, whom you'll meet again in chapter 6, "If You Want to Stay at Home," took her fourth career break when she had her baby.

Will you let age define your career break?

In my view, there is no perfect age to take a career break. As long as you are in reasonable health, age should not be a barrier to enjoying the experience of a lifetime. In fact, many volunteer projects welcome the experience, focus and maturity that mature travellers offer. Later in the book you'll meet Rosie Pebble (61) and Christine Hill (59) who didn't let age stand in their way of undertaking volunteer projects abroad and truly experiencing something they would have never dreamed possible and which has changed their lives forever.

Raleigh International Volunteer Programmes, based in London, not only provide programmes for people aged seventeen through twenty-four, they offer volunteer manager programmes aimed at those who are twenty-five and over. Each expedition requires between twenty-five and forty volunteer managers who bring a variety of skills to lead expeditions or support projects from field bases. These volunteers work alongside country directors and up to 120 young people. Their role is to make sure their volunteer projects are safe, successful, and run to a high standard (www.raleighinternational.org/our-expeditions/aged-25-and-over).

According to yoursabbatical.com (www.yoursabbatical.com/learn/employees/faqs/), here's what sabbaticals bring to each generation:

- Veterans (b.1922–1945): Sabbaticals provide opportunities for senior executives to strengthen leadership teams and mentor individuals through the work coverage process, creating a legacy of leadership.

- Boomers (b.1946–1964): These "knowledge-transfer agents" have an unsurpassed work ethic. Repeat sabbaticals will keep this critical group energized as they stay committed to the workforce and redefine our notions of retirement.

- Gen X (b. 1965–1980): For these "free agents," success means having a career and a life. Sabbaticals are one way companies invest in these relationships and keep them engaged.

- Gen Y (b.1981–2000): The most educated and diverse generation in the workforce, the Millennials are dually driven by career and life goals. Sabbaticals meet their desire for experience and achievement.

When you read the career break and sabbatical stories throughout the book, you'll see that the age of the career breakers profiled varies from twenty-three through sixty-one. Age has not been a barrier to any of these people, nor should you allow it to be a barrier for you. I believe it's all in your attitude, not your date of birth. You can experience anything you want at any age! Just remember that "you'll be a long time looking at the lid!"

Quick story. A few years ago I did an overland trip with Intrepid from Singapore to Bangkok, through Malaysia. Most of the travellers were aged between twenty-two and thirty-eight; however, one man on the trip, George, was sixty-eight. I think I was more surprised that someone of his age wanted to travel with a bunch of people so much younger than he, not to mention staying in hotels and guesthouses that were of a backpacker standard. This didn't seem to bother George, as he integrated with the group really well, participated in all the activities and, in fact, was more active than the rest of us. Whilst we tended to be in a bar somewhere, enjoying the local beverages, he was off exploring the local sites and what the towns had to offer. Whilst George wasn't on a career break as such, even though he only worked six months of the year, the point is that he didn't let age stop him from enjoying his life and experiencing as much as he possibly could.

In summary, there is no right or wrong time when it comes to organising your career break. Considering all the elements mentioned above, the timing depends on your personal circumstances and when you feel it's most appropriate. What's important is that you feel a certain level of comfort about your decision and ensure you are in a position to achieve everything you desire. You may face some challenges along the way; however, I trust this book will provide you with strategies to overcome them and help you make the break you've been waiting for.

Chapter 3:

GETTING CLEAR

Your Big *Why*!

If there's one thing I've learned through the years, it's that if you don't have the right *mind-set*, you will never achieve your goals. At some point in your life you may have wanted something, such as a new car, a new job, a promotion, or to start your own business, but something got in your way that paralysed you from taking any action. Maybe you didn't believe in yourself; or maybe your family and friends told you that you couldn't do it; or maybe you just didn't know how to get started, so you quickly gave up. If this is sounding all too familiar, then I assure you, you are not alone. These reasons, and so many more, stop people every day from attaining their dreams, passions, and desires. Let's not add you to the statistics of people who remain paralysed, and instead move you from a place of *effect* (not making decisions or taking any action or responsibility) to *cause* (making decisions, taking action, and accepting responsibility). For some of us, making the break stays only a dream, as we don't take the time to really think about *why* we want to make the break or, in fact, make any changes in our lives. It's often been said that people's greatest fear is not remaining the same. One thing in life we know is a given is change (along with death and taxes, but let's not spoil things!).

Sometimes people take a career break to travel, not because they want to, but because they are running away from something. If this sounds familiar, then you may want to ask yourself if going abroad is a good decision at this point in time. At the end of the day, it's your life and you can choose what you want to do; however, you need to be honest with yourself and address why you really want to take time out. If it's because you have been looked over for promotion in your job, are experiencing relationship difficulties, or are feeling depressed, then maybe it isn't the right time to make the break. We all know that regardless of where we are physically in the world, our problems follow us, and if you make a break with the weight of the world on your shoulders, don't forget that your shoulders are coming with you!

It can be a very big step to take a career break, and you should be comfortable with your reason(s) for doing so. After all, there may well be a good reason why you have been passed over for promotion or are experiencing relationship difficulties or are depressed, and perhaps you should address those reasons rather than run away from them.

Ronan Flood, from Dublin, Ireland, is a seasoned traveller and has spent the majority of his travels on group tours. Ronan was on a tour from Buenos Aires to Rio de Janeiro, and on the first night, after a few drinks, everyone loosened up and shared a bit about themselves, which is pretty normal when travelling with groups. To Ronan it was obvious his tour guide had run away from something, as she didn't seem cut out for the role. A few nights later, over quite a few more drinks, she disclosed that she came home from work one night to find her friend having an affair with her husband. She subsequently separated from her husband, went on a tour to South America, and enjoyed it so much she then signed up as a tour guide. Whilst initially she ran away to clear her head and escape the situation, by staying away and taking on the role as a tour guide, it was no longer a case of escapism, as her problems and issues still plagued her and impacted her ability to do her job. It's important to remember that a holiday is a holiday and a career break is something entirely different, especially if you choose to work. If your head isn't in the right space, this will impact your experience.

If you empathize with Ronan's tour guide's experience, then it might be best to put your plans on hold for a short time. Once you've sorted things out, you'll have a much better mind-set to steam ahead with your career break plans and really enjoy your experience. Remember, it's important that you make a break for the right reasons.

So what are your reasons?

Why do you want to take a career break?

*What is your big **why**?*

Before you create your big *why*, I'd like to share with you my second career break's big *why*: my family—my parents, my sister, and her four children, who at the time were between five and thirteen years of age. I had been living and working in the UK for ten years and had returned to Australia for only a few fleeting visits, so didn't really get to spend quality time with them. I knew I wanted to spend an indefinite amount of time back in Australia; therefore, I knew I needed a substantial amount of money to sustain my break, as I didn't plan on working. So what did I do? I created what I liked to call my UK Exit Strategy, whereby I designed a budget and spent two years saving. When I felt I had enough money to feel secure and comfortable, I resigned from my job. I then engaged the services of an estate agent to manage my flat and of course made all the necessary calls to the Inland Revenue (tax) and cancelled my utilities. My personal belongings I placed in storage (also known as my aunt and uncle's garage), and I spent the last two weeks prior to leaving catching up with friends and family. At the time I had no preconceptions about my break, other than spending time with my family. My parents and my sister knew I was coming home, though they decided to keep it a secret from the kids, so when I walked through the door one Saturday morning, they got a surprise. It was lovely to be greeted with hugs and big smiles, just as an auntie should be!

My big *why* was so strong that I actually lived with my sister and her family for seven months (call me crazy!). I literally went from living by myself in a flat in London to sharing a house with a family of six, plus me, with only one bathroom and one toilet. I certainly had some situations to adapt to, and quickly. For example, I could never understand why food disappeared from the cupboard so quickly and why I kept finding "floaties" in the toilet! Didn't take me long to learn.

As well as spending time with my family, I reconnected with many friends who I had either gone to school with or worked with, in addition to completing a professional qualification and further personal development study, travelling through parts of Australia, and spending three months in Asia. My carefully planned financial situation allowed me to do all this, and I ended up achieving so much more than I'd originally thought. I fully appreciate how privileged I was to experience what I did. I can honestly say the experience changed me for the better.

If I were to share a moral of the story it would be – *if your why is big enough, you will find a way to achieve your dream.*

Now it's your turn to create your big *why*. If you haven't thought about it before, that's okay; just take your time and really consider what's driving you to take a career break.

In the space below, write down *why* you want to take a career break.

_____

_____

_____

_____

_____

_____

_____

_____

_____

_____

_____

_____

_____

_____

_____

_____

_____

_____

_____

_____

_____

_____

_____

_____

Congratulations on creating your big why!

How do you feel?

_____

_____

_____

_____

Did something come up that you hadn't thought of before?

_____

_____

_____

_____

What are you now telling yourself?

_____

_____

_____

_____

What could hold you back from achieving your big *why*?

_____

_____

_____

_____

How will you overcome these obstacles?

_____

_____

_____

_____

Reviewing Your Values

When was the last time you thought about what you *valued* in life? Is it your family, relationships, trust, integrity, fun, wealth creation, freedom, or financial security? Or all of these?

Most of our values were established when we were young and were learnt from our parents, family members, teachers, and other authoritative figures. However, and this may come as a surprise, we don't have to keep the same values throughout our entire lives—we have the power to change them, and you've probably been doing this already on an unconscious or conscious level over the years.

What are values? To put it simply, values are *the things that are important to you.*

Our values drive our behaviours, and our behaviours drive our results. So if you're not experiencing the results you want in life, then it's time to review your values. I'm guessing that if you want to take a career break, then your values have already started to change. So what do you do now?

To help you with this exercise, I've provided a personal example below. When I initially completed this exercise, in 2008/2009 (prior to my second career break), these were my top ten values.

1. Family
2. Freedom
3. Travel/Adventure
4. Financial security
5. Achievement
6. Efficiency
7. Creativity
8. Friendships
9. Integrity
10. Health

Family became my number one value for 2009 and the basis of all my decisions. As described earlier in my big *why*, I spent two years saving and planning my UK Exit Strategy, resigned from my job, said farewell to my friends and my life in London, and flew back to Australia to spend quality time with my family. I also achieved my second and third values, freedom and travel/adventure, as I chose not to work when I arrived in Australia and therefore had all the freedom in the world to spend my time with whom I wanted and doing what I wanted. Later in the year, I spent three months travelling through Asia and therefore fulfilled my value of travel/adventure. My value of financial security was being met by ensuring I had enough funds in the bank to achieve what I wanted. Finally, my fifth value of achievement was being met as I achieved everything I had worked towards and more.

As time progressed, however, it became apparent that I wanted different things. So what did I do then? I reflected on my values once again and created a new top ten list that included some new values and some of the old ones. I changed some of my values because my life goals had changed. For example, I wanted to write this book; therefore, I needed to be creative. To bring the book to life in terms of developing, networking, and marketing, I needed to be resourceful. To write the book I required freedom, in the form of time. Of course, I have every intention of the book being highly successful; therefore, wealth creation was also in my top four. Let's not forget my fifth value, travel/adventure, as for me, that's what life is all about!

Current top 10 (in order of importance)

1. Creativity
2. Resourcefulness
3. Freedom
4. Wealth creation
5. Travel/Adventure
6. Spirit/Inspiration
7. Passion
8. Friendships

9. Commitment

10. Relationships

Changing my values didn't mean I just threw away the old ones. It's not like I'm just going to stop valuing or ignoring my family. It simply means I'm choosing to focus on other aspects of my life, giving them more priority, and changing my behaviours, actions, and decisions, as my goals have now changed.

Using the same strategy described above, in the space over the page, list your *top 10 values* as they stand *today*. You will be tempted to write them as you *want* them to be, but the aim of the exercise is for you to be brutally honest and write them as they actually are.

To help you, a list of potential values has been provided. Use some of these or add your own.

Professionalism	Adaptability	Achievement
Communication	Positive attitude	Ethics
Honesty	Education & learning	Community
Trust	Recognition	Security
Travel & Adventure	Flexibility	Fulfilment
Respect	Independence	Freedom
Passion	Excitement	Challenge
Dedication	Stability	Drive
Commitment	Responsibility	Autonomy
Efficiency	Creativity	Enthusiasm
Resourcefulness	Change & variety	Enjoyment
Motivation	Financial success	Teamwork & Collaboration
Fun	Integrity	Social Responsibility
Friendships	Determination	Financial Stability

Your *current* top 10 values

Remember to write them as they *are*, not how you want them to be.

1. _____
2. _____
3. _____
4. _____
5. _____
6. _____
7. _____
8. _____
9. _____
10. _____

If any of the values you listed above are *not* serving you or are *not* getting you the results you're looking for, then it's time to abandon them and introduce some new ones. There's no point beating yourself up if you're unhappy with what you identified; just see it as an opportunity to create new values that will serve you in attaining your goal(s).

With your goal of taking a career break, what values do you need to introduce to achieve your desired results? You may find that some of your current values and new ones are the same, as you saw with mine, and if they are producing the results you're looking for, then by all means keep them. In order of importance, now list your new top ten values below.

Your new top 10 values

1. _____
2. _____
3. _____
4. _____

5. _____

6. _____

7. _____

8. _____

9. _____

10. _____

How do you feel about them?

_____

_____

_____

Were there any surprises for you?

_____

_____

_____

What was one of the biggest realisations you made and why?

_____

_____

_____

How do you think your top five new values will impact your lifestyle and the decisions you now make with regard to your goal of taking a career break?

_____

_____

_____

_____

_____

_____

_____

_____

_____

_____

_____

_____

_____

_____

_____

_____

_____

_____

_____

_____

_____

_____

_____

_____

_____

Chapter 4:
MAKING IT HAPPEN

Mind over Matter

If you let your fears, negative thoughts, emotions, and limiting beliefs take control of you, they will stop you from taking action and being successful in attaining your goals. To achieve your goals, you may need to change your mind-set to create positive self-talk. Thinking about taking a career break, for whatever reasons, might take you out of your comfort zone and challenge you in areas you've not experienced before, as we saw with Tracey Baldwyn, who took over four years to finally make the break. If you start to experience negative self-talk, there is a quick and simple method to address this; it's called *reframing*.

So, what is reframing? Reframing is about being aware of what you tell yourself and making the conscious decision to reframe your thoughts into new thoughts that are resourceful, are able to sustain you, and will support you in creating a positive outcome. Here are some examples.

Negative mind-set	Positive mind-set
I can't save the money.	What if I could save the money? What would be possible?
I don't know what to do.	What if I did know what to do? What would I be able to achieve?
Taking a career break is impossible.	How could taking a career break become possible? What do I need to do?

Taking a career break will negatively impact my career.	How could taking a career break positively impact my career?
I could never quit my job.	If I did quit my job, what could I gain?

Considering both negative and positive thoughts before making an important decision is a logical way of coming to a conclusion about what action you are prepared to take. You are the only person who can change your thoughts from negative to positive, and from this, who knows what you're capable of achieving. Your drive, determination, and your big *why* will keep your dreams alive and bring your career break to fruition.

If at any point you start talking or thinking negatively, write down your thoughts in the first column below. Then write down your new *reframed* thoughts in the middle column, and in the third what this new positive mind-set will give you. This will open up your mind to the possibilities of what you can achieve. Here's an example.

Current Negative Mind-set	New Positive Mind-set	What It Will Give Me
I can't save the money.	What if I could save the money? What would be possible?	A feeling of fulfilment A sense of satisfaction Happiness and joy Financial freedom

What Can Hold You Back from Taking a Career Break?

A common culprit in holding people back from taking a career break or sabbatical, or achieving their goals, are their limiting beliefs. But what are beliefs? According to Youell and Youell "Our beliefs are a set of rules that we take to be 'true': rules about ourselves, other people and how the world works. Our beliefs are usually a generalisation about relationships or meaning. We are not born with beliefs. We learn our beliefs. They develop over time as we entertain thoughts, build up our store of experiences and notice patterns. What you believe has a profound effect on how you behave and how you experience the world through your perceptions" (pg47).

Below are some examples of beliefs:

- Rich people are happy.
- The world is a dangerous place.
- If I work long hours I will be rewarded.
- Everything comes to those who wait.
- If I don't make an effort, nothing will ever change.
- If I'm honest, other people will also be honest.
- It's safer to go out in the day time.
- If someone is late, they don't respect my time.

- Everyone should act with integrity.
- If I'm generous, people will like me more.

Our values are supported by beliefs and whilst we have a set of core beliefs, some of these may be limiting beliefs. Limiting beliefs, as described by the Coaching Academy, "are those things you believe about yourself that place limitations on your abilities. Limiting beliefs are simply assumptions that are not true. In order for our actions to have the greatest positive effect, we need to have beliefs that are as close to reality as possible—deceiving ourselves will take us further from our goals. So, a limiting belief, when it comes down to it, is a belief that isn't true."

Top ten human limiting beliefs:

- We fear greatness.
- We fear failure.
- We fear we are not good enough to achieve what we want.
- We fear not being loved.
- We fear rejection.
- We have negative attributes assigned to rich people—rich people are ...
- We fear success.
- We don't deserve/we're not worthy of success.
- We have to work very hard, long hours for our money.
- There are lots of deep-rooted beliefs that hold me back.

(http://www.the-coaching-academy.com/life-personal-performance-coaching/articles/limiting-beliefs.asp).

So where do limiting beliefs come from? Limiting beliefs come from childhood experiences and influences such as our parents, authoritative figures, cultural influences, society, expectations, and coping mechanisms. Have you ever wondered why you believe something to be true, such as "I have to work really hard and long hours to earn money"? It's possible that you hold this belief because you saw your parents working really hard and long hours to support you and your family, and now you've chosen to believe this is the only way you can earn money. Or if you believe that you have to do everything yourself and that you can't rely on others to help you, then maybe as a child your parents raised you to be independent, and from this you now find it difficult to ask for help or trust other people. If you're single, do you put it down to not having met the right person yet, or do you hold limiting beliefs about love, worthiness, and acceptance?

To illustrate this a little further, let's just say you don't think you are very smart and have chosen to believe this from a very young age because someone repeatedly and persistently called you stupid. This has led you to believe that you are, in fact, stupid, and collected evidence to support this belief over the years. As you believed this to be true, you may have failed your exams at school, didn't even bother to apply for university as your grades were not good enough, accepted jobs that didn't challenge you or earn you decent wages, ended up in unhappy relationships, and so much more. In essence, if you believe you're stupid, you will behave and act stupid because *you* believe this to be true. It's quite an interesting concept how limiting beliefs can have a profound impact on the outcome of your life!

On the flip side, if you had chosen to believe "I'm smart" your life may have turned out very differently; for example, you may have excelled at school, achieved top grades at university, started a successful career, earned a good income, and attracted an equally successful partner.

Experiencing events in your life when young, you may have told yourself things that became part of your belief system and have manifested in various ways that have not supported you in attaining your goals, whether they be career, relationship, travel, financial, or career break goals.

The following exercise will examine some of your own limiting beliefs. This may be a difficult exercise for some, as it delves into parts of you that may challenge your comfort zone; it may identify some personal beliefs that you've pushed far back into your subconscious, and it may be an emotional experience to tackle them. The good news is that you are capable of changing your limiting beliefs into powerful statements that will support and sustain you, and we will do this towards the end of this exercise.

In the space below, write three of your limiting beliefs that may hold you back from taking a career break or sabbatical. To make the most out of this exercise, it's important to be as honest as possible.

1. _____
   _____
   _____
   _____

2. _____
   _____
   _____
   _____

3. _____
   _____
   _____
   _____

How do you feel?

_____
_____
_____

Did anything unexpected arise?

_____
_____
_____

How are you now viewing your personal beliefs?

_____

_____

_____

You may have found that some of your personal beliefs evoked negative emotions and painful memories, but just remember that they are true only if you choose them to be true. Instead of getting angry or frustrated or feeling guilty, let's change your limiting beliefs into empowering statements that will change your inner and outer worlds. By doing so, people may start treating you in a different way and you may even start seeing yourself in a different light. Would that make a difference in your life?

Let's work on an example:

If one of your limiting beliefs is "I don't *deserve* a career break because [I don't work hard enough, others around me deserve one more than me, my parents couldn't afford one and therefore I don't deserve to take one either, and so forth]," then it might be worth thinking of the reasons why you have chosen to believe this. Does it go back to your childhood where you felt you didn't deserve to be loved by your parents? Or that you felt you didn't deserve a place at university? Or that you didn't deserve your promotion? It may be that you now believe you don't deserve a career break, as you feel you haven't earned it.

Limiting beliefs have the power (if you let them) to keep you from moving forward and attaining your goals. However, you *do* have the power to change them. You can simply change this belief to "I *do* deserve a career break." From this you can now collect evidence to support that you do, in fact, *deserve* a career break, such as: you deserved to be loved by your parents as you are a kind, caring, and generous person; you earned good grades at school and your place at university through hard work and determination; you deserve your successful career and your promotion as a result of your hard work and commitment; and *now* you deserve to allow yourself to take a career break.

The focus here is to collect *evidence*, and this can come from any area of your life.

When creating your statements, use positive words and avoid using the words *not* and *don't*. Life coach Rachel Anastasi states that "the subconscious mind does not hear a negative word first." A simple example of this is when someone says "Don't forget the keys." What do you do? Forget the keys! The subconscious mind does not process the word 'don't' first and therefore the command your brain hears is 'forget the keys'. I am sure you can think of other examples where this has happened, and all you need to do is change your statements to the positive.

Using the three limiting beliefs you identified earlier, now turn them into new empowering beliefs, also noting down your evidence.

Limiting belief

_____

New empowering belief

_____

Evidence

1. _____
2. _____
3. _____

★ ★ ★ ★ ★ ★ ★ ★ ★ ★

Limiting belief

_____

New empowering belief

_____

Evidence

1. _____
2. _____
3. _____

★ ★ ★ ★ ★ ★ ★ ★ ★ ★

Limiting belief

_____

New empowering belief

_____

Evidence

1. _____
2. _____
3. _____

★ ★ ★ ★ ★ ★ ★ ★ ★ ★

The final step is to embed your new empowering beliefs, and you can do this in many ways, such as:

- Stand in front of the mirror every day and say them out loud (make sure you look yourself in your eyes as you do).
- Make changes in your behaviour through your actions.
- Write your new beliefs on paper and stick them to your mirror or computer.
- Write them in your journal and read them three times a day.
- Say them out loud to a friend, and keep saying them until you sound so convincing that he or she believes you.
- Say them to yourself on the bus, on the train, or in your car.

You may find it difficult to turn off your *inner voice*, so your limiting beliefs keep trying to take over. If you find this occurring, the most important thing is to be aware of it quickly; then start reminding yourself of your new beliefs. The more you say them, the more you will believe them, and the more they will be true! Remember, the choice is yours! The more you embed them into your subconscious, the greater the chance that you will achieve a positive outcome.

It may be that after completing this exercise you would like to work with a professional coach or cognitive behavioural psychologist, and I commend you if you have recognised this and chosen to take action. See below for some resources to help you find a coaching professional:

- **Find a Life Coach** – www.findalifecoach.co.uk
- **The Career Coach** – www.thecareercoach.co.uk
- **Eye 2 Eye Development** – alyse@eye2eyedev.com
- **The Coaching Academy** – http://www.the-coaching-academy.com
- **Free to Be Me Life Coaching** – http://www.freetobemecoaching.com.au
- **The Coaching Institute** – http://www.thecoachinginstitute.com.au

If you wish to find out more on limiting beliefs, here are some websites to help you:

- **4 steps to free yourself from limiting beliefs** –http:// psychcentral.com/blog/archives/2010/07/21/4-steps-to-free-yourself-from-limiting-beliefs
- **Limiting Beliefs – how to recognise them and get rid of them** – http://www.personal-development-coach.net/limiting-beliefs.html
- **Limiting Beliefs** – http://www.the-coaching-academy.com/life-personal-performance-coaching/articles/limiting-beliefs.asp

How are you feeling?

_____

_____

_____

What are you now telling yourself?

_____

_____

_____

Knowing what you know now, how will this impact your life?

_____

_____

_____

Congratulations on completing these exercises. You can repeat them for any area of your life, then monitor the changes and see if you start noticing improvements.

Create Your Goals

"Goal setting is a powerful process for thinking about your ideal future and for motivating yourself to turn your vision of the future into a reality" (http://www.mindtools.com/page6.html). With this in mind, the next step is for you to work on setting some goals to really cement your career break dreams and bring the results you're looking for into your experience.

Goals can be created for every part of your life, such as finances, relationships, family, career, and so many more. However, as we're focussing on your impending career break, we're going to create some goals around this topic. First of all, let's review what goal setting will give you.

- Provides clarity as to the direction you're going
- Stops excuses
- Eradicates pointless activities
- Creates excitement around you as people admire your commitment
- Stops procrastination
- Builds your self-esteem to keep you going
- Maintains your motivation
- Provides you with a sense of direction
- Keeps you on track

There are many goal-setting models available; I've chosen to use the SMART model. This is a very simple and straightforward goal-setting strategy. The acronym makes it easy to ensure all elements of great goal-setting have been covered.

S - Specific

M - Measurable

A - Attractive

R - Realistic

T - Timed

Source: The Coaching Institute, Melbourne (Australia)

What do these mean?

- **Specific** – your unconscious mind loves specificity and responds well when you know exactly what you want and when.

- **Measurable** – if it's measurable, you'll know whether you're on track. By including a date, it keeps you focused.

- **Attractive** – the more attractive you make your goal, the more you're inclined to achieve it.

- **Realistic** – by keeping it realistic, you're more inclined to achieve it.

- **Timed** – ensure your goal has a time frame around it. The deadline will kick new ideas and opportunities into place sooner.

The key to writing a goal is to write what you *do* want, not what you *don't* want. For example, if you want a new boyfriend/girlfriend, you focus on the aspects you want, such as; you want him/her to be ambitious, have a strong character, a great sense of humour, to be kind, generous, loving, and so on. You wouldn't write, "I don't want a lazy boyfriend/girlfriend" or "I don't want him/her to smoke." Remember, what you focus on is what you get, and if you're focussing on what you don't want, you're likely to attract it into your experience. So, with this in mind, we'll only use positive words, and focus on what we *do* want.

The SMART model teaches us to write our goal as if we've already attained it. This way it brings it into our existence as if we've already achieved it.

For example –

It's the first of January [insert year], and I've just checked my bank account. Since I made the decision to travel during my career break, I've saved in excess of £10,000/$15,000. I am so excited and proud of what I've achieved. I am grateful for the love and support of family who have been there for me every step of the way. I can't wait to go to the travel agent and book my flights!

***For example* –**

It's the first of October [insert year] and I've just been awarded my Teaching English as a Foreign Language (TEFL) qualification. Since making the decision to study and enhance my education I now see endless possibilities for my future. My new qualification allows me to teach anywhere in the world. I am so proud of my achievement and all my hard work has paid off.

Don't worry about *how* you're going to attain it at the moment. We'll cover this shortly in "Keys to Achieving your Outcome."

When creating your goal, use words that describe:

- Your vision
- How you feel
- What others would say to you
- What you would say to yourself

So, it's time to write your career break/sabbatical goal. I'll even help you out!

It's _____ [insert date)]

and I have / I am

_____

_____

_____

_____

_____

Everyone is saying

_____

_____

_____

_____

_____

I feel

_____

_____

_____

_____

_____

Let's do one more. Stay focused on your career break/sabbatical goal, but make it about a different aspect, such as finances, a specific destination, or an experience you want to have.

It's _____ [insert date)]

and I have / I am

_____

_____

_____

_____

_____

Everyone is saying

_____

_____

_____

_____

_____

I feel

_____

_____

_____

_____

_____

Keys to achieving your outcome

There are some foundations to goal setting that can really make a difference in your results. The creators of the SMART model noticed that the people who achieved their goals tended to do some things more than those who didn't.

1. Know your outcome

Too many people know what they *don't* want and don't have any clue what they *do* want. They forget they had goals and they settle for the business of everyday life. Know your outcome and you'll have a target to hit. Get really clear about what it is you want to achieve today, in the short term and in the long term. Be clear about why you show up each day, what you want to achieve, and what you want to feel, see, say, and do.

2. Take action

Nothing can replace your getting up off the couch, turning off the TV or whatever else distracts you, and doing something. Nothing can ever take the place of massive action that you do *consistently*. You have the power to choose, and you can choose to act today. Create your budget, start your vision board, or book that open-day event. Remember, the more prepared and informed you are, the better your experience will be. I have a saying (belief!): "If you don't make an effort, nothing will ever change." By taking action, you are making the necessary changes that will bring you closer to your goal.

3. Be observant

One of the master keys to success is to notice whether or not your actions are moving you in the direction of your goals. Is what you're doing keeping you on track or driving you off track? Is this action now moving you in the direction of your dreams and goals?

Many people start something that becomes an unquestioned habit, and before they know it, time has gone and goals are missed. We need to be self-aware, ask questions of ourselves to ensure we're on track, and demand honesty from ourselves about the answer.

4. Be flexible

If we're off track, we need to have the behavioural flexibility to get ourselves back on track by altering the direction of our actions. Maybe we need to stop doing something altogether, maybe we need to tweak an action, or maybe we need to get advice on how to do things differently. Having the behavioural flexibility to alter actions is the difference that makes the difference. Following on from that, if it doesn't work one way, do something else. And if that doesn't work, try something else. And if *that* action doesn't move you closer to your goals, adjust again, and again, and again.

Source: The Coaching Institute, Melbourne (Australia)

The next exercise is to take the goals you created and include the four *keys to achieving your outcome. For example, we'll use one of the goals noted earlier:*

Goal

It's the first of January [insert year], and I've just checked my bank account. Since I made the decision to travel during my career break, I've saved in excess of £10,000/$15,000. I am so excited and proud of what I've achieved. I am grateful for the love and support of family who have been there for me every step of the way. I can't wait to go to the travel agent and book my flights!

Know your outcome

- *To achieve a bank account balance in excess of £10,000/$15,000 by 1ˢᵗ January [insert date]*

Take Action

- *Set up a 'savings account'*
- *Create a budget and review monthly*
- *Organise a funds transfer of £500/$775 or £1000/$1550 per month into my savings account*
- *Note in my diary the day the transfer occurs*
- *Tell a family member or friend, to share my achievement*

Be observant

- *Each month review my savings plan to determine whether it's meeting my goal*
- *Review how I'm spending all my money, and adjust if I can save more*
- *Celebrate my success of becoming closer to attaining my goal*

Be flexible

- *Alter funds transfer payments if necessary*
- *Acknowledge that I might not be able to save every month due to other life occurrences or unforeseen financial commitments*

Now it's your turn. Using one of the goals you created, include the keys to achieving your outcome.

Your goal

_____

_____

_____

_____

_____

Know your outcome

_____

_____

_____

_____

_____

Take action

_____

_____

_____

_____

_____

Be observant

_____

_____

_____

_____

_____

Be flexible

_____

_____

_____

_____

_____

Great work!

How do you feel?

_____

_____

_____

What are you telling yourself?

_____

_____

_____

As we all know, and have probably experienced, life can sometimes throw little surprises our way which may get in the way of achieving our goal(s). Therefore, you may need to create some strategies to overcome them.

List five things that could get in the way of you achieving your goal(s).

1. _____

2. _____

3. _____

4. _____

5. _____

How do you plan to overcome them?

1. _____

2. _____

3. _____

4. _____

5. _____

At some point during this process, you may need support from your friends and family to help keep you on track to ensure you achieve your goals. It's important to surround yourself with people who will provide you with the right encouragement, love, support—and maybe a good kick up the butt to keep you focused. You may even wish to ask a family member or friend to be your accountability buddy to really help keep you on track.

If you don't create the right support network, you may fall back into old habits that do not serve your new goal(s) or your desire to fulfil your dreams. With this in mind,

Whom do you need to support you in achieving your goal(s)?

1. _____

2. _____

3. _____

Fantastic! You are now highly skilled at writing goals and creating keys to achieving your outcome. You have also successfully covered how to manage any obstacles that could get in your way of achieving your results and identified who is in your support network to help keep you on track.

If it helps you maintain focus, write these goals out so they are in your view all the time—maybe stick them on the fridge or in your diary. This way they will be a constant reminder and help you stay committed to taking action. If you're a visual person, you may even want to include some pictures to keep you inspired. Would a picture of the Amalfi Coast in Italy keep you motivated? Or a photo of the Great Wall of China? Or a baby sea lion from the Galapagos Islands? Why not create a photo collage and hang it in your room? Visualise what it's going to be like when you're finally there.

Be, Do, Have!

You're about to embark on an epic journey, one that will require many skills, complete focus, and an abundance of energy. With all of these, you'll be armed with the necessary tools to turn your career break dream into a reality. Let's bring it home by completing the following exercise.

Who do you need to *be* to bring this experience into your life?
(For example, you might need to be determined, strong, disciplined.)

_____

_____

_____

_____

_____

_____

_____

_____

_____

What do you need to *do* to achieve your goals?
(For example, you might need to create a budget, buy a wall planner, and cut down on spending.)

_____

_____

_____

_____

_____

_____

_____

_____

_____

What do you want to *have* before, during, and after your career break experience?
(For example, you might want to have the support of your family and friends, have opportunities to meet some fantastic people, and albums full of photos to remind you of your experience.)

_____

_____

_____

_____

_____

_____

_____

_____

_____

Chapter 5:

IF YOU WANT TO TRAVEL

Travel is the most popular way to spend a career break, and it's important to identify your *travel style* and your preferred *type of travel* before spending your hard-earned money and embarking on the unknown. There are so many elements to consider, and identifying these before you go may help you avoid uncomfortable situations or circumstances and ensure you spend your money on experiences you want to have to maximise your enjoyment.

What Is Your Travel Style?

As defined by Answers.com, the world's leading Q&A site, travel can be described as "to go from one place to another" or "to pass or journey over or through." Style is "the way in which something is said, done, expressed or performed" (thefreedictionary.com). Therefore, your *travel style* could be interpreted as the way in which you "do" and "express" yourself through and during your travels. So, before you determine your travel style, here are some things to consider:

- Do you like flush toilets?
- Do you like group travel?
- How much can you carry?
- Do you like extreme sports?
- Are you a loner?

- Do you get motion sickness?
- How do you handle the heat?
- Do you prefer five-star luxury or sleeping under the stars?
- Are you comfortable sharing a bathroom?
- How would you feel if your preferred type of food or drink wasn't available?
- Would you be willing to respect cultural dress?
- Do you like camping?
- Are you interested in "responsible travel"?
- Do you like sharing a room or a tent with a stranger?
- Can you swim?
- Do you pick up languages easily, or would you be willing to try?
- Will you need to take medication with you?
- How will you feel about visiting villages where people live in challenging conditions?
- Do you like to blow-dry your hair every day?
- How do you handle the cold?
- Do you prefer room service?
- Do you like to see all the sights?
- Will you need assistance getting up and down stairs?
- Can you be seen without makeup?
- Do you like to drink a lot of alcohol?
- Do you like interacting with local people?
- Are you a chatty person or a quiet, reserved person?
- Do you like carrying around a backpack?
- Do you want to learn about other cultures?
- Do you have any illnesses that will impact your experience?
- How would you feel if the person you were sharing a room with snored every night?

- Are you comfortable sleeping in hard beds, soft beds, on hut floors?
- How do you handle travelling for long periods of time?
- Do you like to carry around a guidebook?
- Would you prefer to sit and drink coffee and watch the world go by?
- Are you an early-morning person?
- Can you sleep under a mosquito net?
- Are you a "go with the flow" person?
- Do you have allergies?
- Are you prepared to wear comfortable shoes rather than fashionable shoes?
- How long can you hold your bladder?
- Do you prefer fine dining or street market stalls?
- Would a structured itinerary make you feel more comfortable?
- How do you feel about long train journeys?
- Do you need to shave every day?
- Would you be willing to visit orphanages and children's homes?
- Do you cope well with bugs, spiders, mosquitoes, and other insects?
- Are you prepared to take medication if required?

That long list is only the tip of the iceberg when determining what style of travel you prefer. You may have found that whilst reading the list you pulled some faces, which means either you liked what you read or you didn't. You may have thought of some of your own. Take a mental note of your answers, or circle the ones you associate with the most, as these will help you decide *where to go*, *what to do*, and *under what circumstances* you'd visit a country. For example, if the idea of sleeping on hut floors with no electricity or running water sounds like an adventure, then head to countries that offer you this kind of experience. If the thought of being around people all the time doesn't appeal to you, then maybe group travel isn't for you. If you suffer from motion sickness, then find alternatives, such as flying between destinations rather than taking long bus trips.

There are pros and cons to both travelling alone and travelling with a friend, as you'll find out soon when you meet Alexis Grant and Gary Davies. If you are thinking of travelling with a friend, then ask yourself the following questions (sourced from my own experience and also King & Robertson, 2004) before embarking on a journey, which could turn into the best adventure of your life or a nightmare from hell.

- *Do you have similar interests?* You don't have to agree on everything, but having similar interests might make your time away more enjoyable, as you can share the memories instead of just showing each other the photos the next day.

- *What's their budget?* The last thing you want to argue about when you're travelling is money. The reason you are travelling with a friend is to share the experience. It will be difficult if one of you can afford to do all the activities you want, while the other is left on the sideline to watch, getting more resentful by the day. Not a recipe for success!

- *Do you have the same amount of travelling time?* The pace at which you travel is important. Having the same amount of time will allow you the flexibility and freedom to fit everything in. If one of you has one year and the other six months, you may end up being rushed along faster than you'd like.

- Are you as tidy (or messy) as each other? If you're a tidy freak (no judgment here), then how will you feel sharing a hut/tent/room with your friend who leaves towels on the floor, orange peels on the bed cover, and clothes all over the place?

- Is your friend normally cheerful and optimistic? The purpose of travelling is to enjoy yourself, experience new cultures, and meet new people, plus create memories to last a lifetime. If you're travelling with someone who is moody, has bouts of depression, and can be pessimistic, think about the impact this will have on your experience. You may be the kind of person who can brush this off, but if you're not, then you may need to rethink who would be your best travel buddy.

- How flexible are you? This is where your travel style will help you identify whether you're a person who is happy to just "go with the flow" or if you're a more structured person and like the idea of a well-planned itinerary. It may be that you can combine both styles, which will keep both styles happy.

Sources: King & Robertson, *The Backpacker's Bible*; Sue Hadden

What will you do if you find yourself in the position of wanting to travel with a friend, but none of them are able to take time off work or they can't afford it, or you may have found someone but they want to travel to different places? Well, you may have to consider travelling solo! There are many travel companies available, such as Intrepid, Gecko, and Gap Year for Grown Ups, who offer a wide range of group travel opportunities for the solo traveller, to locations all around the world. You'll meet like-minded people, set out on a predetermined itinerary, be provided with a local tour guide, have all your transport and accommodation taken care of, enjoy the safety of travelling with a group, and so much more. This might sound like the ideal experience for you; however, ask yourself this question: "Will this type of trip give me the freedom and flexibility I'm looking for?'"

If you're looking for more flexibility in terms of where you go, how long you stay somewhere, and what you do, then travelling solo may be your best option. For some, this might sound quite daunting, but it wasn't for journalist and social media coach Alexis Grant, from Washington, D.C., who embraced the freedom and the challenge of travelling solo through West Africa, Cameroon, and Madagascar in 2008 at the age of twenty-seven. Alexis figured she would meet more people travelling solo (she says this turned out to be true!) and would be able to follow her own whims without worrying about anyone else. She also knew the chances were slim that she'd find a companion who would want to go to Africa for six months, since for most of her friends it would mean leaving a job. Upon this realisation, it wasn't long before Alexis quit her reporting job, threw on her backpack, and ventured into the world of the unknown with a sense that her adventure and the experiences she would take away were going to have a lifelong effect on her, both personally and professionally.

Determining where you want to go will have an impact on whether you decide to travel solo. Having spent a semester abroad in Cameroon during college, Alexis knew she wanted to go back there to visit her host family. Then she simply looked for French-speaking countries. To Alexis it seemed logical to hit a bunch of countries while she was in West Africa, so she travelled overland through Senegal, Mali, Burkina Faso, and Ghana. Visiting Madagascar had always been a dream of hers, and she was keen to get at least one "dream" destination on her itinerary!

Even though you may have done your research on the places or countries you want to visit, it might not be until you arrive somewhere and get a feel for a place that you can determine how long you plan to stay. Prior to her departure, Alexis set up a loose itinerary and bought her flights, so she knew she had to get to, for example, Ghana by a certain time to catch her flight to Cameroon. So she would let herself stay in one place for a while if it interested her or if she had a purpose there, for example, writing a newspaper story, since she freelanced along the way. But she purposely gave herself more time than she figured she would want in each place so she wouldn't feel rushed. She also changed her itinerary several times, because she didn't have to adhere to anyone else's schedule.

Whilst there are advantages to travelling solo, Alexis also recognises some of the drawbacks, which include experiencing occasional loneliness, lacking the safety of a partner, and having to pay what she calls the "single tax"—in many places, the price of the room is the same whether you've got one person staying there or two. Females may thus have to take extra precautions if travelling alone. Some of her suggestions are outlined below.

1. Befriend local women.
2. Book a bed for the first night.

3. Bring only what you can *easily* carry.

4. Carry food.

5. Also carry a book.

6. Expect to pay more than couples.

7. Look for roommates.

8. Consider wearing a (fake) wedding ring.

9. Make an effort to be friendly.

Alexis says that "most risks kick up a notch when you go it alone." If you want to read more about her nine tips above to help you be more prepared, visit her blog (http://alexisgrant.com/2011/01/11/9-tips-for-women-traveling-alone). If you're looking for more tips on independent travelling, such as asking for the cheapest room, buying visas along the way, and packing a pillow, then visit this page of Alexis's blog: http://alexisgrant.com/2010/05/05/a-dozen-tips-for-independent-travelers.

Reflecting on her experience, she notes she would have liked to have put more work into prepping her blog and freelance contacts, so she could have spent less time in internet cafés. She would also have packed less; she ended up ditching some of her belongings along the way. Overall, her trip was more than Alexis had hoped for!

When Alexis returned home, she began penning her adventures with the intention of publishing her own book sharing her personal experiences, trials and tribulations of backpacking solo through Africa. Alexis says her book will be "full of both adventure and introspection, satisfyingly real, freeing readers from the fairy-tale love that drives most modern-day travel".

Gary Davies, from Somerset, UK, has taken two career breaks over the last few years. During his first career break he travelled with friends, and the second time he travelled alone. Gary says he enjoyed sharing his first travel experience with two very close friends. They were all reasonably laid-back people and approached travelling with a certain amount of flexibility. There were no major arguments and, when needed, they all compromised with minimal fuss. However, Gary noted that while they were lucky in that they enjoyed other people's company, at times they also enjoyed their own company and preferred a little solitude. Summing up, Gary states "we all concur we all had an amazing time and the memories will last forever."

Gary chose to travel alone on his second career break, which made the experience very different, yet equally enjoyable. He found that he met more people when travelling alone, as he had to make more of an effort to start a conversation; but before too long, talking to strangers felt perfectly normal. Gary also observed that as a lone traveller he was often invited to join fellow travellers, locals, or ex-pats for a beer or a game of cards, and that this happened less frequently when he travelled in a group.

Back in 2009 I travelled through Vietnam on a group tour where we spent many hours each day on our tour bus driving to each destination. Historically, I had never experienced any issues with travelling on buses, or any form of transport. However, this one particular day, the road was very windy and for hours it felt like we were on a roller-coaster ride. I felt so sick I had to ask the bus driver to stop so I could step off and get some fresh air. I was quite embarrassed (and I don't embarrass easily) as everyone was looking at me through the windows, wondering whether I was going to throw up. Not really the kind of attention I wanted as a lone traveller! This was the first time I had ever experienced motion sickness, and it continued through my following travels in Laos and Cambodia. Great! Just what you want when you're travelling through countries where they drive like maniacs and don't understand the concept of "road rules." Worse, the motion sickness tablets I started taking made me feel like I was in some kind of vortex, and it took me ages to feel normal again. Knowing this, when booking my future travels, I now have to seriously consider the type of transport and condition of the roads, as I don't fancy being ill every time I step on a bus or get in a car – and I'm sure my fellow travellers would agree!

When Ronan Flood travelled independently through Northern Argentina, he stayed in a hostel that offered a variety of tours. On the first day he met an Irish girl who was travelling with her friend. It was her first time backpacking and also her first time in South America. Her friend had backpacked extensively all over the world and was used to staying in hostels and making her own travel arrangements.

During his conversations with the Irish girl, Ronan quickly realised she was not cut out for backpacking, as she seemed completely shell-shocked and unprepared for travelling in a country where limited English was spoken. Two days later he met the girl in the hostel again, where she was anxiously trying to book a flight to get her home as soon as possible. She told Ronan it just wasn't working out for her. Ronan believes that if she'd been better prepared, in terms of researching the country in more detail, the languages spoken and the type and level of transport and accommodation provided, her situation could have been avoided, and she would not be heading home early filled with disappointment.

To ensure you are fully prepared before you go, the exercises below are designed to help you identify your *preferred style of travel*. Write down in the space below, what you think your *preferences* would be when travelling, such as: group travel, flying between destinations, standard of accommodation (e.g., five-star hotels), etc.

1. _____

2. _____

3. _____

4. _____

5. _____

Furthermore, there may be some personal items or effects that you can and can't live without. For example, I drink vanilla tea and have been drinking the same brand for over 13 years. When I go abroad, I take packets of vanilla tea with me and during my second career break I purchased many packets off the company website and had them posted out to me in Australia. So, it's fair to say I can't live without my vanilla tea. What I can live without is make-up. I actually enjoy not wearing make-up every day and allowing my skin to breathe. It actually gives me a sense of freedom.

In the space provided, list what you can and can't live without.

What can you live without?

1. _____
2. _____
3. _____
4. _____
5. _____

What can't you live without?

1. _____
2. _____
3. _____
4. _____
5. _____

Hopefully, these lists, examples, and exercises have given you something to think about and will help you clarify and identify what *style of travel* is best suited to you. Maybe you've realised you can't live without your hair straighteners, your Starbucks coffee in the mornings, or keeping in contact with your friends and family on a daily basis. Or maybe you've realised you can live with wearing the same clothes a few days in a row, looking "au naturel" all day every day, and sharing a room with someone you've never met. It may be that you've now ruled out some of the experiences you thought you wanted, or you've included some you never thought you would ever consider. If you're looking to push yourself out of your comfort zone during your travels or just test the waters, then hopefully you have identified some areas that will enable you to achieve this.

Most travel companies will offer you choices with regard to *style of travel* and are often linked to your budget, your circumstances, and the experiences you wish to have. To help you even further, below are some travel options available to you:

1. Adventure
2. Comfort
3. Budget
4. Family

Let's go into more detail.

1) *Adventure Travel,* could be described as any activity where a certain level of active participation is required. But what does that mean to you? An excuse to wear a cravat? A reason to swing through jungles? Or maybe be chased through the streets of Spain by a raging bull? Whatever your definition of adventure, there are plenty of activities to whet your appetite.

Adventure travel may include:

- *Safaris.* Get up close and personal with lions, zebras, and orang-utans!
- *Walking.* Not to be taken lightly. Walking can be taken very seriously and many adventure-walking holidays have been created for this purpose, not to mention the host of products on the market, such as professional walking sticks. It's nothing to poke a stick at – ha ha, get it?
- *Activity and adrenaline.* Bungee jumping, sky diving, white water rafting, diving with sharks (come face-to-face with a Great White), or even rock climbing.
- *Trekking and hiking.* Check with your tour company before booking a trekking or hiking trip to ascertain the level of fitness required. If you have to carry your packs, there may be local guides you can hire to carry them for you.
- *Expeditions.* When I hear the word *expeditions,* I automatically think of the North Pole. However, there are lots of expeditions to many other destinations, so no need to rush out and buy a stack of thermal underwear and a ticket to the Arctic.

- *Festivals and events*. These are a great way to learn about and interact with another culture. There is something for everyone, whether it's chocolate festivals in Perugia, Italy, the Rio Carnival in Rio de Janeiro, or a full moon party in Thailand.

- *Kayaking*. A fun activity for the whole family or go it solo. At your own pace, glide through the water and enjoy the peacefulness of nature.

- *Cycling*. Jump on a bike and feel the wind through your hair … or your helmet. A certain level of physical fitness may be required, depending on the type of trip.

Travel companies offering a variety of adventures include:

- **Activities Abroad, The Activity Travel Company** – www.activitiesabroad.com
- **Exodus** – www.exodus.co.uk
- **Imaginative Traveller** – www.imaginative-traveller.com
- **Gap Adventures** – www.gapadventures.com

2) *Comfort*. When you think of comfort, do you think first-class flights, five-star hotels, gourmet food, expensive wines, and private cars to transport you to each destination? Comfort travel doesn't have to mean compromising on experiencing the local cultures; in fact, comfort travel may be all the things listed above. However, it may equally be just spending a little bit more on better hotels or guesthouses, private transport, and flying between destinations as opposed to long overland bus trips. If you can afford it, why not?

Travel companies offering a variety of comfort travel include:

- Intrepid Travel – www.intrepidtravel.com
- Comfort Travel (Canada) – www.comforttravel.ca
- Discover China Tours – www.discoverchinatours.com
- Comfort Safaris – www.comfortsafaris.com

3) *Budget.* Travelling on a budget means spending as little money as possible during your trip. The word *budget* might invoke thoughts of sleeping in a room with eleven other people, sharing a bathroom, sitting on a bus for eight hours with your knees under your chin and the bus won't stop for toilet breaks (this happened to Ann Sullivan when she travelled through India), cooking in a communal kitchen, or sleeping on a train holding your backpack – and you'd be absolutely right.

Budget travellers tend to seek out the most inexpensive means of transportation, food, and accommodation; however, budget travel is nothing to be sniffed at. If you really want to get down with the local culture, meet some interesting and intriguing people, not to mention enjoy the feeling of freedom, then budget travel could be for you. Budget travel tends to attract the younger generation, though it does not discriminate against the older (but wiser) generation. Typically, younger people tend to have less money and are more eager to meet other travellers to share their experiences; therefore, budget travel may be their best or only option.

Travel companies offering a variety of budget travel include:

- **Intrepid Travel** – www.intrepidtravel.com
- **Gecko's Adventures** – www.geckosadventures.com
- **Real Gap** – www.realgap.co.uk
- **Gap Year** – www.gapyear.com

4) *Family.* Of course, this depends on whether you have a family and, if so, you plan to travel with them. Family adventures give you (the parent) and your children the opportunity to share an experience and discover the world together. Think of how many slide nights you can have when you get home! (Do you remember slides, or am I just showing my age?)

The travel industry has responded to the ever-increasing demand for family travel, with the creation of companies that specialise in family-specific or family-friendly adventures.

Travel companies offering a variety of family travel include:

- **Intrepid Travel** – www.intrepidtravel.com
- **Peregrine Adventures** – www.peregrineadventures.com
- **The Adventure Company** – www.adventurecompany.co.uk
- **Travelmood Adventures** – www.travelmoodadventures.com

Now that you've started identifying your style of travel, is there one in particular that stands out for you? Or could you see yourself combining a couple of styles? In the space below, note your top two styles.

1. _____
2. _____

If one of your top styles is *adventure*, note any activities that particularly appeal to you in the space below.

1. _____
2. _____
3. _____
4. _____
5. _____

Before settling on your travel style(s), here are a few more things to consider:

- Can you afford your preferred style(s)?
- Would you prefer to travel alone or in a group?
- Is/Are your preferred style(s) going to give you the experience you desire?
- If you're travelling with someone, is their preferred style the same as yours?
- What are you willing to compromise on?

What Type of Travel Experience Is Right for You?

There are a host of different types of travel experiences available to you, and your travel style will determine what type of travel experience you're drawn to. From completing the exercise on identifying your travel style, you may have already recognised what sort of experience you're looking for and what is more suited to you. However, if you're still gathering ideas, suggestions, and information, then here are some travel experiences available to you:

- General travel
- Responsible tourism
- Volunteer work
- Working abroad (paid)
- Work experience (unpaid)
- Learning a new skill or a new language
- Gaining a professional qualification

Let's look at these in more detail.

General Travel

As we've already seen, according to the research conducted by Santander, travelling during a career break is the most popular plan when taking time out (www.everyinvestor.co.uk/personal-finance/savings/recession-drives-spike-in-gap-years-and-sabbatical). So, if you're looking to visit lots of different countries, learn about other cultures, attend festivals and events, meet new and interesting people, or try something new, then general travel may just be for you. Gary Davies spent one of his career breaks in South East Asia, travelling through Thailand, Laos, and Cambodia. Gary says, "I found when arriving somewhere for the first time, not knowing anyone or where anything was, gave me a real sense of excitement and adventure." During one of Gary's nights out, some of the locals invited him to join them at a discotheque. He said it wasn't what he expected, as it was more like a theatre with tables and seats out in front of a stage. A live band was playing a combination of pop/

rock music and traditional Issan (North East Thailand) music. Gary joined in the festivities and danced alongside his new local friends but states that he "was bopping around, probably looking quite ridiculous and certainly standing out being the only westerner in the club. A few of the women tried to teach me some of their traditional Thai dance moves, but even though they gave me the thumbs up, I knew I was failing miserably. We continued to dance, chat, and drink until the late hours. I eventually said my good-byes and caught a taxi back to my hotel." Getting involved in local activities and trying, even if failing, to communicate with the locals will give you greater exposure to the culture of another country, plus its traditions, its people, and its customs. You may find yourself, like Gary, enjoying a night out and making some new friends.

During a hill-tribe trek in northern Thailand, Bal Mudhar , and the others on her Intrepid group tour spent the morning playing with the children from a local school. The guys on the trip challenged the local boys to a game of football, which they loved. However, the girls played games a little less "physical." Bal recalls, "The kids were allowed to come out of class to spend time with us, and they just seemed so happy we visited their school. We played games like 'duck-duck-goose' and 'ring-a-ring-a-rosie,' which I hadn't played in years. It certainly took me back to my childhood days. It was such a great experience, and I still tell my friends about it to this day."

Responsible Tourism

When booking your break with travel agents or when speaking with tour guides, you may hear the term *responsible travel*. So what does this mean? According to Intrepid (www.intrepidtravel.com), responsible travel is "a style of travel that is environmentally, culturally and socially responsible. Travelling this way means contributing more directly to local economies and having more opportunities to meet the locals." More and more travel companies are adopting this philosophy, including Gecko Adventures (www.geckosadventures.com), who state that environmental and cultural sensitivity is important to them and that they are constantly learning more and informing their clients how best to enjoy their travel experience without impinging on the regions they travel through. They offset their carbon emissions with gold standard schemes for both their trips and the wider organization.

Responsible tourism has become so important that in 2004 responsibletravel.com (the world's leading travel agent for responsible travel) founded the Responsible Tourism Awards, in partnership with the *Metro* newspaper, *Geographical Magazine,* and the World Travel Market. Virgin Holidays became the headline sponsors in 2007, with the award aptly being named Virgin Holiday Responsible Tourism Award (www.responsibletourismawards.com). Over the nine years, the awards have attracted more than 11,000 nominations from fifty-five countries around the world. Nominations are accepted from organisations worldwide that believe they are leading the way in responsible tourism. The award covers categories such as Best Hotel, Best in a Mountain Environment, Best for Poverty Reduction, and many more.

Ed Scott, the managing director of AVIVA, a company that specialises in volunteering in South Africa, believes volunteerism is an excellent example of responsible tourism. He states that "international volunteers leave their mark in South Africa, not only by dedicating their time and energy to a community or conservation project, but also through the positive contribution they make in supporting local businesses, tourism operators, craftsmen and women, and the many jobs that are created and sustained by purchases they make, and activities they take part in while they are here. When managed correctly, volunteerism ticks all the boxes when it comes to satisfying the criteria for *responsible tourism,* bringing visitors to areas of the country outside the traditional tourist routes, and providing a sustainable means for NGO (non-governmental organisations) projects to develop and employ local people".

If travelling is for you, then adopting a responsible travel philosophy will enhance your experience, as you will be supporting and interacting with local cultures, meeting people from the community, and engaging in local customs and traditions.

Intrepid identified seven tips for being a responsible traveller:

1. Learn as much as you can about the country you're visiting: its religion(s), values, customs, and rules.

2. Pay particular attention to appropriate behaviour, dress, and body language.

3. Learn some of the local language, and don't be afraid to use it – even simply saying hello can help break the ice!

4. Always ask before taking photos of people, and offer to send back copies if possible.

5. Minimize your water and energy use.

6. Avoid activities that involve the mistreatment of animals or that promote the exploitation of endangered species.

7. Support local business by purchasing locally made products, food, arts, and crafts rather than imported products.

Find out more about being a responsible traveller at www.intrepidtravel.com/responsibletravel.

Thailand-born Nutty Nithi owns and manages two travel companies, Nutty's Adventures (www.nutty-adventures.com) and Ayutthaya Boat and Travel (www.ayutthaya-boat.com/ABT/index.php) based out of Ayutthaya, one hour north of Bangkok, Thailand. Nutty and his team are passionate about responsible tourism and community-based tourism (CBT) and adopt this philosophy and approach in all of their tours and programmes.

In the words of Nutty, "tourism services and activities are planned and managed by local people, working together in a 'CBT Group.' Tourism programmes are especially designed to support community and environmental projects, to build local skills and to distribute opportunities fairly. Guests experience and learn about rural people, their lives, cultures, and inter-relationships with the natural world." In a quick Q&A with Nutty, here's what he says about CBT.

Why is CBT so important to you?

- We always think of sharing benefit among tourism industry and local communities. Community-based tourism (CBT) is used as a community development tool. Nutty's Adventures is unique as it is managed and owned by the community, for the community, with the purpose of enabling visitors to increase their awareness and learn about the community and local ways of life.

What are the benefits for the local community?

- CBT was initiated for tourism that takes environmental, social, and cultural sustainability into account.

What do you believe travellers get from this experience?

- Tourism services and activities are planned and managed by local people, working together in a "CBT Group." Tourism programs are especially designed to support community and environmental projects, to build local skills, and to distribute opportunities fairly. Guests experience and learn about rural people, their lives, cultures, and inter-relationships with the natural world. Nutty's Adventures hope that this will increase respect for local cultures and the environment among hosts and guests.

Nutty's Adventures offer "Destination Adventurous Excursions." With Nutty's CBT trips, guests have an opportunity to experience and learn about the community and the environment through fun, hands-on activities, led by local community guides. These include jungle trekking, hand-weaving clothes with natural dyeing colours, cooking lessons, and so much more. Nutty's Adventures hope that this will increase respect for local cultures and the environment among hosts and guests.

Volunteer Work

What is volunteering?

According to Joe Bindloss, "volunteering is choosing to offer your efforts, energy and expertise for free. Some volunteers want to make a lasting difference in the world. Others are looking for a life-changing experience. For many it's a reaction to modern-day materialism. Whatever your motivation, doing something to make the world a better place is likely to be an experience that stays with you for the rest of your life" (Bindloss "Volunteering").

Why do people volunteer?

Volunteering is a popular way to spend career breaks or sabbaticals. During this chapter you will meet many individuals who have spent either their entire career break or a portion volunteering on various projects such as marine conservation, teaching in schools or working in hospitals. You will also meet some career break professionals who provide details on career break options, contribute their views and opinions on volunteering, including the benefits of volunteering, and share their own experiences.

In an interview with Ed Scott of AVIVA, he shared with me the reasons why people volunteer, the qualities and mind-set required of a volunteer, and the invaluable skills volunteers can bring to their projects.

Career breakers join AVIVA for various reasons, with many looking to do something fulfilling and worthwhile that will either help them with future career choices or allow them time to rejuvenate by doing something they are passionate about, before returning to their current job, or one in a similar line of work. Many career breakers join them to take in new life experiences, meet new friends from around the world, interact with local people, and of course to combine all this with free time to take in the wide range of activities and attractions that South Africa offers.

Although the personal benefits of volunteering, for you, as a "career breaker" are many, it is equally important for you to understand why you are making the choice to volunteer, and to take some time to examine your motives for volunteering. It is also important to assess the impact that your stay will have on the wildlife and children you encounter. You will not change the world in one visit, but they have seen that contributions from many volunteers over a period of time produce the best results for the children and wildlife in the care of well-structured projects.

If you have a genuine desire to help others less fortunate than yourself, and wish to do so in a responsible way, then this is a good indication that you already have many of the qualities needed to undertake this kind of immersive life experience.

As a career breaker, you already have a wealth of knowledge and transferable skills that are invaluable to many projects. Your energy and enthusiasm are equally valuable and can help to provide fresh impetus or introduce fresh ideas to a project. The majority of non-profit wildlife and community projects in South Africa receive little or no government funding, and are reliant on the good will of local and international volunteers to get the work done. Whilst local volunteers typically are able to help out on an ad hoc basis to fit in around their full-time position, international volunteers play a crucial role in being able to commit to a set period of time.

Ed sums up by sharing what he expects from a typical volunteer:

- Open to experiencing new cultures and meeting people from around the world
- Tolerant and respectful of others, no matter what their beliefs or background
- Looking forward to broadening their horizons and exploring new lands
- Flexible and able to adapt well to new situations and environment
- Self-disciplined with a sense of independence

- Recognising that volunteering provides them with a rewarding way in which to develop their own personal qualities and character while giving something back to the environment and communities in need
- Pro-active and looking for opportunities to experience their new surroundings
- Acknowledgement that South Africa in many ways is still a developing country that will provide them with a wide range of new experiences

Just how popular is volunteering?

Richard Nimmo is the managing director of Blue Ventures, a marine conservation project. He comments on the change in the number of people taking career breaks and notes that while in 2008 they experienced record numbers of career breakers, 2009 and 2010 have been more difficult. However, he says, he has seen an increase in interest in 2011 and hopes that people are beginning to have the confidence again to take extended breaks from their jobs and join volunteer projects. Richard says that he tends to receive applications and communications from career breakers who already have an interest in the marine environment and want to add to that, or from those who are intent on a career change and see the opportunity of working with them as an important part of that change in gaining experience and testing their assumption that marine conservation is for them.

Sophie Pell, from Raleigh International, noticed a slight decrease in the percentage of volunteers taking time off for a career break or to consider other options between 2009 and 2010, from 52 percent to 45 percent. However, she noticed a slight increase of those taking a sabbatical, from 31 percent to 34 percent. Mark Jacobs, managing director of Azafady, sends some 150 volunteers to Madagascar every year, with an average age of twenty-four. Mark observed an increase in the number of volunteers over the last few years but has also noticed the typical length of time spent on projects has decreased from three months to four or five weeks. Mark believes this trend is due to an unlimited number of volunteer options existing in the market and that people like to experience more than one. Furthermore, people have less time and are not always in a position to take three months off to join their Pioneer programme. Therefore, Azafady created a shorter programme aimed specifically at people in this position, to ensure they had access to their volunteer programme.

Ed Scott, AVIVA, reported a steady increase in the number of volunteers travelling to South Africa, with a proportional increase in career breakers amongst these. Social media such as Facebook and Twitter have played a role in making more people aware of the volunteering's positive impact on personal growth, and the wide range of experiences involved in well-structured volunteer programmes.

Since 2002 AVIVA have been fortunate to host volunteers from fifty-seven countries worldwide, including the UK, the USA, Australia, Canada, the Netherlands, Germany, Norway, Vietnam, India, Peru, Japan, France, and many more. Along with career breakers, they have hosted volunteers from a wide range of other backgrounds, including students, teachers, nurses, pilots, doctors, vets, retirees, policewomen, lawyers, and social workers, to name just a few.

What is interesting is that 84 percent of volunteers are female, and Ed confirms that this percentage has remained nearly the same since 2002. Below, Ed gives the age range of those undertaking AVIVA projects.

- 38% are aged between 16 and 20 years
- 32% are aged between 21 and 25 years
- 18% are aged between 26 and 35 years
- 7% are aged between 36 and 45 years
- 5% are aged 46+
- The eldest volunteer so far was 72.

Overall, the majority of career breakers fall within the 26–45 year category, and this percentage has increased from 16 percent in 2003, to 25 percent in 2010.

Benefits of volunteering

There are many benefits to volunteering, both personally and professionally. Of course, the extent to which you benefit from your experience will depend on the type of project you selected to undertake, the value you intend to gain, and of course the attitude you take with you. According to AVIVA, these benefits include:

- Making a direct contribution to a worthwhile cause
- Adding an impressive and unusual contribution to your CV/resume
- Having an opportunity to discover your own hidden talents
- Developing your own character, confidence, and abilities
- Seeing the world from a global perspective
- Meeting like-minded people from around the world
- Experiencing new cultures and lifestyles
- Enjoying a great, fun experience with lasting memories
- Participating in a wide range of spare-time activities
- Having an experience that goes beyond tourism
- Potentially helping you decide on your future studies or career choices

(www.aviva-sa.com/frequently-asked-questions-detail.php?id=5)

AVIVA carried out an independent study, over a two-year period, evaluating the effects of volunteering on AVIVA volunteers in South Africa. In summary, the results revealed significant changes in six traits in the AVIVA volunteers, in comparison to a control group. The volunteers displayed significant decreases in depression, anxiety, and vulnerability, and increases in emotionality, adventurousness, and assertiveness. The authors use the results to claim that volunteering in South Africa is good for you! To read the full report, visit http://www.aviva-sa.com/files/mytrip/Research-Paper-International-Volunteering.pdf.

Types of volunteering

The purpose of this section is to help you make a more informed decision as to the most appropriate volunteering option for you. You can choose from:

1. sourcing a volunteering project yourself when you arrive in your desired country;
2. sourcing a volunteer project from an "independent volunteering" organisation; or
3. sourcing a volunteer project through a "placement agency"

What's the difference?

1) Sourcing a volunteering project yourself when you arrive in your desired country

This option gives you the freedom and flexibility to source a volunteer opportunity when you arrive in your desired country. This may be the cheapest option and may even be free.

Back in 2005 I walked into a children's home in a small village outside of Ei-lan, Taiwan, expecting to be greeted by energetic toddlers running around causing chaos. To my surprise, the manager pointed me in the direction of babies. I literally stopped in my tracks, thinking "Babies! I don't do babies!" For some reason, when I considered volunteering during my first career break, working with babies didn't come into the picture, but here I was, faced with nine babies, ranging from two days to nine months old, all needing to be fed, burped, changed, and cuddled. Even though this was out of my comfort zone, I was up for the challenge.

This opportunity had come about through a friend of the friends I was staying within Ei-lan. I had expressed an interest in doing some volunteer work, so the next day, their friend picked me up and drove me to the home, about twenty minutes from where I was staying. He had been to the home many times and on every occasion made a personal donation. He introduced me to the managers, who were

American, though they spoke fluent Taiwanese and Chinese, and had been managing the home on and off for over twenty years. They made me feel very welcome and accepted my offer to volunteer, then proceeded to show me around the home.

One of the challenges I faced was actually getting to the home each day. I didn't have a car, so my friend, Samantha, loaned me a scooter. This may sound easy to those who've driven a scooter, but this was new to me, and a bit scary. After a quick thirty-minute lesson (Samantha wasn't a very patient teacher), I was out and about driving on the roads and negotiating the local traffic. Now that I had the confidence to drive a scooter, I had to actually find the home by myself. Again, this may seem easy, though where I was staying, and typical of Taiwan, there were many rice fields, and they all seemed to look the same. It was literally, "Turn left at the rice field, go around the round-a-bout, then turn right at the next rice field." It was very easy to get lost, but whilst this was a challenge, it was also part of the adventure. I felt free, alive, and energised every time I drove to the home. The beautiful scenery, the reflections of the rice fields, and the welcome I received each morning from the manager and other volunteers are precious memories.

Over the course of the next month, I learnt the many skills attributed to caring for babies (including changing dirty nappies) and found the experience one of the most rewarding, fun, and memorable to this day. The other volunteers lived on site, and as they didn't have transport, they weren't able to leave the home very often. So on my way every morning I would stop at the local convenience store and pick up snack foods, drinks, and other treats I thought they would like. Maybe this was why they liked me so much!

After telling my mum about my experience, she hand-made the children's home a quilt to keep the babies warm at night (my mum is a Queensland Quilter, and even I have to admit she is amazing!). The manager of the home loved it so much that they hung it on the wall as a reminder of the time I was there and of the generous contribution made by my mum. Even six years after this experience, I still think about the babies I helped care for, and knowing they were adopted into loving, caring homes gives me a great deal of comfort.

2) *Sourcing a volunteer project from an "independent volunteering" organisation*

Richard Nimmo offers us some insight, advice, and guidance about independent volunteering and Blue Ventures: "Organised volunteering can provide structure, safety, accountability and reassurance for participants and families. In addition a UK-based volunteering organisation has to abide by certain guidelines, must have liability insurance and the volunteer can take legal recourse if there is a problem or a dispute."

He adds, "There are good and bad providers in every industry, you often get what you pay for and a few well targeted questions and a little research by a volunteer amongst volunteering organisations will easily and quickly establish an organisation's credentials and motives. Organisations that are members of associations such as the Year Out Group (www.yearoutgroup.org) or who abide by British standards (http://www.bsigroup.com/en/sectorsandservices/Forms/ BS-88482007/FAQs-for-BS-8848/) provide tested and regularly assessed standards that should provide well-structured experiences for volunteers."

Stephen Knight, of Volunteer Latin America (www. volunteerlatinamerica.com), defines independent volunteering as "doing volunteer work without working through or having the support of a third party." He believes that independent volunteering is the most ethical form of volunteering, as "any money paid goes entirely to the cause rather than into the pockets of a third party." He also argues that it is much cheaper and more satisfying to organise your own placement; however, it is essential that you research the area and project thoroughly. There are a number of websites that connect independent volunteers to free and low-cost volunteer projects, such as Volunteer Latin America and Volunteer Work Thailand.

Original Volunteers (www.originalvolunteers.co.uk) is an independent volunteer organisation that specializes in overseas placements for volunteers, offering them at a fraction of the cost of the larger companies. Check out their website for more details.

Another organisation that specializes in supporting grass-roots communities is Azafady (madagascar.co.uk), which offers a wide range of volunteer projects in Madagascar, with an overall aim to "eradicate poverty, suffering and environmental damage in Madagascar."

In November 2007 Azafady won the Best Volunteering Organisation category of the Virgin Holidays Responsible Tourism Awards, having been rated Highly Recommended in this category in 2005. The organisers commended Azafady for "demonstrating real achievements, meeting the locally defined needs of communities in Madagascar and for producing detailed reports on impacts and being transparent about where the volunteers' money goes." The award further cemented Azafady's reputation as a leader in the field (http://www.madagascar.co.uk/getinvolved/pioneer.htm).

Like Original Volunteers, Azafady is led by the requirements and needs of the villagers and is not owned by a larger conglomerate. The staff live on site, and people from the surrounding villages approach Azafady and ask for their assistance in, for example, building a school in their village. Eighty local staff are employed, which benefits the local community and their families. As there are so many good causes, when a local approaches Azafady, their request is placed on a waiting list. This approach ensures that the right projects are selected and local needs are taken into consideration.

Azafady volunteers certainly make a significant contribution to local communities, but they are also provided with an extraordinary and memorable experience. Information on the volunteer programmes offered by Azafady and more specialist placements can be found via the "Get Involved" tab on their website (http://www.madagascar.co.uk/getinvolved/index.htm), or for volunteer feedback and more information on the opportunities offered by Azafady, visit http://azafady.us/blog/ and www.facebook.com/AzafadyMadagascar.

Xaali O'Reilly Berkeley, from London, recognised that finishing school can be an exciting point in a young person's life. For many it's a first recognisable achievement, a first qualification, a step into the "real" world. Which is why it can also be quite daunting. What next ... work? University? All of a sudden you have to make decisions that are likely to affect the rest of your life. But at seventeen or eighteen, you're not always sure of what you want to do for the rest of your life, where you want to end up, or – if you do know – how to get there. So bring on the gap year!

Many students in the UK take a gap year even if they do have a pretty clear idea of how they want to proceed in life; it gives them a chance to take a break from education and see the world while they are still young, especially as they can't be sure the chance will come again. For others it's a chance to try different things, which may help them decide which road to continue down.

The latter was the case for Xaali. She had just finished studying for her baccalaureate and was unsure whether to pursue a future in natural sciences, as she had always intended, or to go down the road of graphic art, not to mention a leaning toward philosophy, her favourite class in baccalaureate.

She decided to look for a part-time job and try different things throughout the year to help her decide, but while surfing the web, she saw a link to a page offering advice and suggestions to students intending to take a gap year. While most ideas were more leisurely than decision-making-orientated, one idea caught Xaali's attention – volunteering abroad.

An infinite number of volunteering opportunities are out there, all over the world and in almost every field you can think of. So much so that, an industry has set up around it, and unfortunately, this is sometimes more business-orientated than entirely committed to the cause they claim to be. However, from Xaali's research, she felt Azafady was different.

Two crucial reasons influenced Xaali's decision to work with Azafady. First of all, the fact that it's a charity-linked NGO – all funds are channelled straight back into work on the ground, where it's needed. But perhaps even more importantly, it doesn't throw aid at people; it doesn't just step in and fix what's broken; it doesn't put up fences around reserves and forbid locals from using their country's natural resources; Azafady helps normal people find ways of improving their lives, making the most of what nature has to offer in a sustainable manner, benefiting people and wildlife, in the hope of ensuring brighter futures for both.

Having decided to volunteer on Azafady's Lemur Venture conservation programme for 4 weeks, Xaali got down to the business of fundraising, for which Azafady provided ample material and assistance, as well as information on every possible aspect that need concern a prospective volunteer travelling to a very different country – not to mention quick and helpful answers to every question Xaali emailed them!

After a month of living in a tent, trekking through the rainforest searching for (and finding) lemurs and other unique creatures, working alongside Malagasy people and learning about their language and culture, Xaali really wasn't ready to go home. But alas! All good things must come to an end, and she has no doubt that her time working with Azafady was the most memorable experience of her life. Not only that, but it helped her decide what path she wanted to follow – and so now she is studying for a Zoology degree so she can dedicate her life to conservation.

Here are some other independent volunteer organisations for your consideration.

- **World-Wide Volunteering** - www.wwv.org.uk
- **Open Mind Projects** – www.openmindprojects.org
- **U Volunteering** - www.uvolunteer.org
- **Ecoteer** – www.ecoteer.com
- **Volunteer Work Thailand** – www.volunteerworkthailand.org
- **Volunteer 4 Africa** – www.volunteer4africa.org

3) Sourcing a volunteer project through a "placement agency"

Projects Abroad programme advisor Craig Ferriman speaks of why using a placement agency is so popular: "We pride ourselves on giving the volunteer all the choices they could need – choice of destination, project, duration, start and finish dates, joining as a(n) individual/pair/group, type of accommodation (host family/hostel), additional travelling time before or after placement and so on." Later in this chapter I cover volunteer costs and what's included; however, for your reference, Craig has provided a breakdown of what's included in the Projects Abroad fees. This will give you a deeper understanding of what goes on behind the scenes to ensure you gain the most from your experience. Here's what's included:

- Food (three meals a day)
- Accommodation (either with local family or shared accommodation with other volunteers)
- Airport transfers (on arrival and departure)
- Insurance (comprehensive luggage and health insurance)
- Secure personal webpage (including pre-departure travel information, project details, accommodation details, visa details, office contacts, insurance details)
- Induction (including visit to Projects Abroad destination office. Briefing on details in handbook)
- Orientation—a tour of where you are based, including transportation, communications, and currency exchange
- Chance to meet volunteers from around the world
- 24-hour in-country staff support throughout stay; project monitoring – staff members assess your status, progress, and health
- Dedicated office in destination
- Organised social activities, e.g., barbecues and dinners

What's not included?

- Flights
- Visa costs
- Spending money

Sophie Pell shares with us Raleigh's unique offering and details why people choose to volunteer with them:

- Expeditions bring people together from all walks of life, meaning that volunteers can spend time with people they wouldn't normally meet. This helps break down social barriers and improves the confidence and communication skills of volunteers, as well as provides the opportunity for people to make friends for life.

- Because of the structure of training and facilitated learning opportunities available to them, volunteers get the opportunity to build confidence and develop soft skills such as leadership and problem solving, which are highly valued by employers.

- Because Raleigh has permanent field bases in each of the countries in which it operates, Raleigh has spent time building relationships with local NGOs, organisations, and communities. This means Raleigh works with the local communities to ensure the projects that volunteers work on are genuinely needed and sustainable. Volunteers can get pride and satisfaction from the fact that they are making a genuine difference.

- Volunteers can gain an in-depth cultural experience, because the communities really want them to be there and welcome them into their homes and villages. This enhances their overall experience and helps them to develop cross-cultural awareness skills.

- Raleigh stays in touch with its alumni and offers opportunities for volunteers to make a difference to society once they've come back from an expedition. Raleigh has developed a network of passionate and dedicated alumni to inspire their peers and communities and to support development efforts.

- Raleigh offers a range of bursaries to support young people from the UK whose personal and financial situation means that they would be unable to raise the full expedition costs. In 2010, 39 percent of young people received financial support from Raleigh in the form of a bursary.

- At Head Office in London, Raleigh staff are available twenty-four hours a day, seven days a week in case of emergencies at home or abroad.

- Because of Raleigh's experience running expeditions, Raleigh represented the Year Out Group in setting up a new British Standard (the BS 8848) for the safe management of overseas ventures. This British Standard provides a rigorous standard for organising and managing visits, fieldwork, expeditions, and adventurous activities outside the United Kingdom. This means that Raleigh is audited every year to ensure they comply with the standard.

Here are some placement agency organisations for your consideration:

- **Raleigh International** – www.raleighinternational.org
- **Projects Abroad** – www.projects-abroad.co.uk
- **AVIVA** – www.aviva-sa.com

In summary, there are a host of opportunities available to you, and whether you choose to go it alone, join an independent volunteer organisation, or volunteer through a placement agency, the decision is totally yours. Choose what you feel comfortable with and what you believe will give you the experience you're looking for. Read the personal stories below, which have been contributed by individuals who have completed volunteer projects across a range of organisations and types of projects, such as conservation, working with children, and working with animals. They will provide you with insight into the project and a realistic view of what to expect and the experiences you can look forward to.

Types of volunteer projects

There is certainly no shortage of volunteer organisations, non-government organizations (NGOs), and charities offering you the opportunity to participate in projects all over the world, some of which are mentioned below. Volunteers are able to select their chosen project and the country where they would like to volunteer and generally spend between two weeks and twelve months working in this capacity. It's important to note that even though you are volunteering your time, services, and hard work, you will have to pay for the experience. For example, two weeks volunteering to work with lion cubs in South Africa could cost you around £1,000, which will include accommodation, food, and project fees. Generally, you would also be expected to cover your flights, visas, insurance, etc. If you wish to extend your stay, there is usually an additional charge. Ask lots of questions and do your research before making a commitment, in order to be fully prepared and minimize any financial surprises.

In the section below, you'll find a range of volunteer projects to give you a taste of what's on offer.

Conservation projects

According to thefreedictionary.com, conservation is "the protection, preservation, management or restoration of wildlife and or natural resources such as forests, soil and water from loss, damage or neglect." Volunteering to work on an environmental or conservation project not only allows you to put something back into the environment that's long lasting, but for many people it's the opportunity to work outdoors in a practical hands-on type of role, where you're often getting your hands dirty whilst enjoying the fresh air. Some find it far more appealing than working from nine to five in an office (www. voluntaryworker.co.uk/environmentalconservationprojects.html).

Conservation projects are offered by many organisations, such as Volunteer Latin America, i-to-i Volunteer and Travel Abroad, Projects Abroad, Raleigh International, Azafady, AVIVA, and many more. You could find yourself helping to preserve the Amazon rainforest in Ecuador, on a diving and marine conservation in Cambodia, working on a reforestation project in Kampung Bowang Jamal, Borneo, or in an eco-development conservation in India.

Blue Ventures (www.blueventures.org) offer marine conservation expeditions specifically aimed at people on a gap year or career break. Through these expeditions, volunteers from around the world work closely with field research teams and in partnership with local communities. They are dedicated to conservation, education, and sustainable development in tropical coastal communities and have been recognised for their commitment to responsible tourism by many awards, including the Virgin Holidays Responsible Tourism, Observer Ethical Awards, IUCN Young Conservationist Award, Conde Nast Traveler Environmental Award, and many more. For further details, visit www.blueventures.org/newsroom/our-awards.

Richard Nimmo has an interesting story to tell about his own volunteer experience with Blue Ventures and how, after participating in a project personally, ended up becoming the managing director. Richard explains that for over ten years he had been working in London in sales and marketing for television and radio stations. He needed a break from his hectic and pressurised work life and also had a strong desire to take some time to see and work in a new environment and challenge himself, as well as make a positive contribution through a conservation project. His friends, family, and partner were all hugely supportive of the idea and his plans. This helped him make the decision to take a break and join Blue Ventures' conservation expedition in Madagascar.

Originally the break was intended to be for two months, but it turned into sixteen months. So how did that happen? Richard volunteered in the Blue Ventures Marine Conservation programme for six weeks from March 2004, and then spent a month travelling in Madagascar. His experiences as a volunteer in Andavadoaka with Blue Ventures and his travels in the rest of Madagascar were extraordinary. He decided that Madagascar was a place he wanted to spend more time.

On returning to the UK in late May of 2004, he applied for the position of expedition leader in Madagascar, was successful, and found himself back there in July, staying until June 2005. Since then he has been the general manager and now holds the position of managing director of Blue Ventures in London. It would be fair to say that Richard said good-bye to his previous career in sales and marketing and has never looked back.

On speaking of the highs and lows of his career break and subsequent move, Richard notes that living and working in a remote community with volunteers from many countries and local people gave him a huge sense of achievement, as they all contributed to a successful and award-winning marine project. Richard sums up his experience by saying that "working and living in Madagascar was a wonderful experience" that has given him "a new focus and an impetus to work in a new sector. Seeing and travelling in another culture is always interesting but to live in a different culture and work there, gives you a deeper insight and understanding."

Jon Palin spent six weeks of his twelve-month career break volunteering through AVIVA with The South African Foundation for the Conservation of Coastal Birds, SANCCOB, (www.sanccob.co.za) in South Africa. He had always loved penguins, so he searched for places where he could gain hands-on experience, and SANCCOB seemed to be the only place that could make use of someone without any specialist zoology/veterinary skills.

Jon says that "it's important to save the lives of African penguin chicks as they are an endangered species due to loss of habitat, oil spills and over-fishing. One hundred years ago there were well over a million of them; now the population is around 50,000. At peak times SANCCOB can have 1% of the entire species on its premises. Adult penguins moult once a year and can't go to sea during that time. And if moulting coincides with the breeding season, then parents can't feed their chicks, and without intervention the chicks would starve." Jon says they are brought in only if they are in real danger in the wild. SANCCOB saves the lives of hundreds of penguins each year.

During his time with SANCCOB, Jon was specifically involved in handling the birds, feeding them fish and tube-feeding them liquids; providing basic medical treatments, such as giving pills, holding them while staff conducted blood tests, and more complex procedures; and of cleaning and disinfecting of pens, pools, and equipment. He also maintained records of their treatment.

Working alongside Jon were a small team of permanent staff members with zoological and veterinary experience, but most of the hands-on work is done by volunteers. Volunteers ranged from gap-year students to retired people. About half were local volunteers based in Cape Town, and the rest international volunteers from around the world. In terms of living in a different country for the duration of his break, Jon says in some ways it's not too different – the suburb of Cape Town he lived in was similar to Europe. However, he never quite got used to the inequality and poverty elsewhere, and living in a house protected by an electric fence felt odd.

During his experience, the main skills Jon learnt included how to handle and treat penguins safely, how to work in a totally different environment and work with a wide range of people. Whilst Jon didn't have a veterinary background, he says the most important quality was a willingness to work hard at whatever was needed that day. After volunteering he had the chance to go on safari and visit Namibia, which he says was wonderful and very different to anything he could see back home.

Simon Ferrier, from London, had been an active scuba diver for about seven years, so when he started looking at travel options, he decided to combine volunteer work with his passion for scuba diving. Simon simply searched the Internet for "diving volunteer work" and came across a conservation and environmental project in Cambodia offered by Projects Abroad. Simon selected Cambodia, as it was less commercial than Thailand, cheaper, and was also an easy location in which to be based, as he wanted to spend half of his career break travelling through South East Asia.

Like Ted Harrington, Simon had been made redundant from the construction industry in December 2009 and thought this would be a great opportunity to travel. He was single and had no responsibilities other than his mortgage, so was left with little reason not to go. One of his friends had travelled around the world seven years earlier and always said that if Simon ever got the opportunity to travel, then he should just do it. And that's exactly what he did.

Simon spent three months volunteering in Cambodia and even spent his forty-fourth birthday on an island. Simon shares his story and brings to life his experiences.

Imagine a tropical island in the middle of a turquoise sea with deserted golden sandy beaches, warm temperatures and blue skies. Hold that thought, because on the island of Koh Rung Samleom you will find all of this and more ... much more. When you wake up in the morning and the sun is shining through the window of your thatched bungalow and you can see the ocean lightly lapping the sand only metres away, you are left thinking that life does not get much better than this.

It is not often that one gets the opportunity to combine some adventure and excitement with helping to conserve and protect some beautiful reefs and its marine life. But my three-month stay on the island will leave a lifelong impression. Mixing with other volunteers from all around the world, all with the one goal ... conservation.

Embracing the simple way of life was easy for me, but it may not be for everyone. Getting away from all the things we take for granted like hot water, internet, phones and showers was a way of exploring yourself and your mindset. Beautiful but basic accommodation is on offer. You do not need more.

The main roles of the volunteers are educating the local village in sustainable fishing methods, which in turn will improve their way of life and food security, and collecting marine data, which will provide the local fishery authorities with information on the health of the reefs and its marine life.

As well as the underwater activities, there are other areas of work to be carried out like beach clean-ups, jungle trekking to monitor rare types of orchids and other plant life, and the building of an incinerator which I helped to start while I was on the island.

The diving is excellent and in my three months on the island I completed over 100 dives. The diving activities include seahorse surveys, reef surveys and reef clean-ups, all of which are planned and organized in a safe manner. Even if you have never dived before, you could not find a better place to learn with qualified, quality instructors who allow you to learn at your own pace.

So change the traditional travelling path for a change of pace and sign up for a minimum of two months to really appreciate and get fully involved in the project. Everyone's input makes a difference.

Richard, Jon, and Simon agree on many of the benefits of volunteering on a conservation or environmental project.

- Your work will have a positive and lasting impact.
- You will learn more about the environment and conservation issues.
- You will improve the lives of locals.
- You will develop new knowledge and skills.
- You will contribute to the preservation of natural beauty.
- Working outdoors can have a positive impact on your mental health.
- It can open doors to a new career in an environmental or conservation capacity.
- Everyone's input makes a difference.

I don't know about you, but I found the stories from Richard, Jon, and Simon all very inspirational; they really convey a flavour as to what you might experience if undertaking a conservation volunteer project. It also seems very clear that they do, in fact, make a difference in the communities where they are volunteering, not to mention making a difference to their own lives at the same time.

Working with children

Do you like the idea of making a difference in a child's life? Do you want to put a smile on a child's face? Maybe you'd like to teach children some of your skills to help them in everyday life. Working with underprivileged, sick, or orphaned children can be a very rewarding experience and is a popular volunteer option. You can choose to work with children in Asia, Africa, South America, and many other locations across the globe. You could be working with AIDS orphans in Kenya, children with special needs in India, or underprivileged children in Argentina; teaching English to children in Ecuador; or volunteering with Buddhist novice monks in Luang Prabang, Laos. Organisations offering volunteer work with children include: i-to-i Volunteer and Travel Abroad, Global Vision International (GVI), Save the Children, MondoChallenge, Action for Children, Barnardo's, and Projects Abroad. Another alternative, if you live in the UK, is to mentor a child through Chance UK (www.chanceuk.com) and really make a difference to a child's life on a longer-term basis.

In 2008, at the age of sixty-one, Rosie Pebble retired from her job as a learning support assistant. More than twenty years earlier, she had been deeply affected by the revolution against communism that swept across Eastern Europe, and she particularly remembered haunting images of children in terrible conditions in Romanian orphanages. For the first time, she felt she was in a position to offer help, so Rosie searched the internet and was drawn to the website of Projects Abroad. After studying their brochure and attending an Open Day, where she spoke with people who had previously volunteered, Rosie boarded a flight (for the first time ever) and headed off to Romania to spend six weeks volunteering in a hospital and six weeks volunteering in an orphanage.

Speaking of the highs of her experience, Rosie says walking into the baby room at the hospital was amazing, as the babies would stand up in their cots and clap and laugh. She also enjoyed giggling with the children in the orphanage, especially when they tried to teach her Romanian. Speaking of the challenges of her volunteer experience, Rosie says the lack of supplies, staff, and hygiene was evident at the hospital. Rosie also said that all the children she worked with are of Gypsy origin, and given the inherent racism against Gypsies in Romania, there is very little chance that they will be adopted. Other challenges included sharing a room with someone she didn't know, getting about and shopping without speaking the language, and coping with a different culture. There were also some hardships to contend with, such as a lack of hot water in her host family's home.

Rosie has been back to Romania twice since, despite having returned to work, and has plans to return for a longer period when she finally retires, permanently.

Health care

Some organisations offer volunteer roles for skilled professionals. For example, Mad Adventurer (madventurer.com) offer volunteer roles to trained health care workers, typically in a district clinic or hospital. Mad Adventurer states, "Facilities and care are under-resourced in every sense and doctors and nurses really value any help that can be given. Working in healthcare in a developing country really presents a totally different set of conditions in which to work and can be a truly rewarding experience" (madventurer.com).

Raleigh International seeks registered doctors, nurses, and paramedics for each of their expeditions to fill their volunteer role of medic and project manager. As a medic, you would be expected to: ensure medical kits are fully stocked, educate the expedition on first aid, document all medical issues, deliver emergency care in remote environments, and promote health throughout. Louise Hyde was working as a doctor in A&E when she applied to join Raleigh's expedition to India as the medic and project manager. Louise wanted to learn new skills and build up her self-confidence, and Raleigh seemed to provide the ideal opportunity to achieve these goals. In addition, she had been looking for the chance to get involved in youth development, see a bit more of the world, and experience life in a completely different culture.

Her main role involved trying to keep everyone safe and healthy while at the same time creating an environment where they could be in control of their own experience. Louise prepared medical kits, visited the local hospital, and organised the staff medical training. She was able to utilise her current medical skills during the expedition, and she also developed her teaching skills, as she set up a health education programme at the local school.

Helen Norton joined Raleigh's expedition in India in 2010 as a medic and project manager. She had previously volunteered with Raleigh in Namibia in 2007, and Borneo in 2009. Helen had been working full-time as an A&E nurse whilst studying part-time for an MSc in Infrastructure in Emergency. She decided to take a year off to get the practical experience she needed for her MSc and to thus put theory into practice. She was also keen to change career direction, moving from A&E and into aid agency work.

As a result of her time with Raleigh, Helen says, she learnt that India is both incredible and overwhelming at the same time. She found that her normal coping mechanisms for dealing with stress were not helpful, and she needed to adapt and learn new ones. Finally, she learnt that the biggest challenges often give the best results and that people can do the most amazing things when faced with fear and challenge.

Working with animals

If you choose to volunteer with animals, you could find yourself swimming with turtles in Greece, working on a marine conservation on the Great Barrier Reef, Australia, studying and conserving jaguars in Costa Rica, or working with orang-utans in Sumatra or with lions in South Africa. With so many options to choose from, it's difficult to make a decision. Most projects of this kind allow you to get up close and personal with the animals you've chosen to work with, and you could be contributing to the preservation of a species and helping to build them a more secure future.

Tamaryn Dryden, based in London, though originally from South Africa, finally lived her childhood dream of volunteering for a wildlife team on a game reserve in South Africa. The main project was the reintroduction of white lions to the wild, but she got involved in all sorts of things, from water buffalo counts, to feeding the hippopotami, to rescuing an injured cheetah. Not only did she work with animals, Tamaryn also learnt to shoot a rifle, conduct game counts, and track animals. With no prior experience, Tamaryn says that "the challenge was working out how you could actually add value rather than just being a spare part." Tamaryn says of the benefits of her experience that "it can be a great opportunity to develop your confidence by putting yourself in new situations. It can also give you a fresh perspective on life in general and any role you have done previously. It can help you identify the things that really matter to you and the future direction you wish to take yourself in. Overcoming new challenges is a skill you can take on to anything, anywhere."

Teaching

Teaching projects are offered by most volunteer organisations in countries such as Asia, Africa, South America, and Eastern Europe. Teaching English is the most popular; however, there are opportunities to get involved in teaching other subjects, such as maths, science, drama, arts, and crafts and sports. You could find yourself teaching children in primary school or secondary school, or maybe even adults. Do you need a professional qualification to teach? This may vary, depending on the organisation you book through and how long you're planning to undertake a teaching project. MondoChallenge (www.mondochallenge.co.uk) don't require any formal qualifications; however, they do provide a teacher training weekend for those wanting to get some idea of how to get started. i-to-i Volunteer and Adventure Travel offer Teaching English as a Foreign Language (TEFL) qualifications, where completing a weekend course will qualify you with the essential skills you need to teach a class overseas. i-to-i Volunteer and Adventure Travel state, "Volunteer teaching abroad will leave you feeling fulfilled in the knowledge that you're making a tremendous impact on the future lives of underprivileged children – it's really a win-win situation!" (http://www.i-to-i.com/volunteer-teaching-english.html). This was certainly the case in 2010 for teacher and artist Christine Hall, who, at the age of fifty-nine, took an "enforced" career break from her teaching job in the UK and, after hearing about Projects Abroad from a friend, signed up to volunteer as a teacher and work for a local newspaper in Addis Ababa, Ethiopia. During her initial research, Christine was open-minded about location; however, she was keen to broaden her horizons and wanted to go where she felt there was great need. Ethiopia fitted the bill perfectly.

Christine stayed with a host family in Addis Ababa and was particularly inspired by her host mother, Astede, who, through sheer determination and the wish to see children in a deprived area have the opportunity to go to school and be educated successfully, set up a school that accommodates over seven hundred pupils and employs thirty teachers. Astede was so inspirational that she was the subject of Christine's first newspaper article, "How a Remarkable Woman Realised her Vision."

Reflecting on her time in Ethiopia, Christine says there was an incredible friendliness about people and that she noticed how people in their sixties commanded great respect from younger people. The people, the laughter, and the sunshine stand out in her mind. Although images of drought and starvation are still indelibly etched on our western minds when we think of Ethiopia, time and change in economic development revealed a very different Ethiopia to Christine.

Law and human rights

Back in June 2009, Natalie Shah watched with dismay as job cuts and redundancies overwhelmed London, and she became acutely aware of the impact that the global recession was having on the legal profession. Having taken out a loan to fund her legal studies – and with no concrete offer of work in the pipeline – she searched for a way to enhance her CV, increase her employability, and make her application stand out from the competition.

Natalie's research led her to Projects Abroad, who offered legal internships all over the world, with each placement specialising in a different area of law. In Mongolia and South Africa, law interns got involved in human rights projects; in Morocco the focus was on children's and women's rights; and Shanghai was the place to go for a more commercial/corporate experience.

By this time Natalie had managed to acquire temporary work in a law firm in London; by coincidence, a colleague's sister had been on a Projects Abroad law internship in Ghana. She told Natalie more about the organisation and put her in touch with a friend of hers who had been to Shanghai as an intern, which gave her some firsthand knowledge of working and living in the city. Everything she heard only increased her desire to go. Finally, Natalie phoned several legal HR departments in London to enquire whether such an experience would add value to her CV, and they all responded positively. So, in September 2009, Natalie flew to Shanghai to join her placement in an intellectual property law firm, where she worked as a paralegal for the next three months.

Natalie's work was diverse and included commenting on recent case law, proofreading legal documents and articles translated from Chinese into English, writing articles for the website, and researching commercial contracts. She gained valuable paralegal experience and learned about the business and cultural practices that are the norm in China. Natalie says that choosing to work as a legal intern in Shanghai not only offered her the opportunity to live and work in another country but also allowed her "to acquire valuable legal experience which was not readily available in the United Kingdom." She says, "This has helped me to progress to my current position, and I once again have an interesting job in a vibrant, cosmopolitan city – this time, London."

Youth work and community development

Some volunteer organisations offer opportunities to work on community-based projects. For example, you could help teach children IT skills, teach dance, volunteer to work with street children, teach music or work on programmes aimed at young offenders. You will have the opportunity to utilize your skills, knowledge and expertise to really help make a difference and contribute to communities across the globe. Raleigh International, Projects Abroad, i-to-i Volunteer and Adventure Travel, MondoChallenge and AVIVA are just some of the organisations that offer a wealth of community-based volunteer projects. Projects Abroad, who offer projects in Mexico, Ghana, Jamaica, and many other countries, state that by becoming a volunteer "you will be contributing towards the preservation of some extraordinary ways of life and working with many local people to achieve a common goal" (http://www. projects-abroad.co.uk/volunteer-projects/community/).   Mad Adventurer go on to say "community development projects give you the chance to really 'give something back' and experience a whole new environment and way of life. The communities they work in are always incredibly hospitable and you will be amazed at what you can experience and achieve and how much difference you can make to a community's life and future" (http://www.madventurer.com).

Euan Platt was a youth worker for a national charity, LGBT Youth Scotland, and studying part-time for a master's in Community Education before joining Raleigh International as a team coach and project manager in Costa Rica and Nicaragua. As part of his master's he was required to complete a three-month voluntary placement, which involved working with young people. Euan saw Raleigh as the perfect opportunity for his placement, as it involved working with young people from a range of different backgrounds in a very hands-on way.

The role involved going out with the young people on the three expedition phases and working with them on various projects. As team coach Euan contributed to the volunteer manager induction training, assisted with venture allocations, and worked more closely with venturers who needed extra support.

Euan explains that as a project manager you have to use and develop a full range of skills. For example, his background in youth work was extremely beneficial when it came to group work, carrying out one-to-ones with venturers and organising games and energiser activities. Raleigh gave Euan the chance to try so many new things and develop more practical skills, such as using a range of tools, building, and navigating. He states that the great thing about Raleigh is that everyone comes with different skills and the volunteers learn lots from each other.

When reminiscing about his time with Raleigh, Euan notes one of his best moments on expedition was at the end of phase one. Their main project contact organised a party in the village to say thank you to his group. Although it was in a very remote location, a large sound system and generator were brought to the village. They all danced with the community and had a really enjoyable evening. Euan says it was just one of the many examples of the amount of effort the locals put into making the group feel welcome and appreciated. Euan sums up by saying that volunteering with Raleigh is challenging and involves a lot of hard work, but it offers you the chance to see incredible parts of the world and meet local people, which would be hard to achieve any other way.

Building

Not a qualified builder? It doesn't matter! According to i-to-i Volunteer and Adventure Travel (www.i-to-i.com), all you need is "enthusiasm, reliability and an appetite for hard work". If you like getting your hands dirty, seeing a project from inception to completion, or bits in between, and really making a difference to underprivileged families and communities, then a volunteer building project may be for you. Not only would you be working alongside other volunteers, you'd be working with members from the community towards a common goal. Mad Adventurers (www.madadventures.com) often employ local skilled tradesmen to help supervise the project and teach volunteers new skills. You could be building a school, people's homes, a much-needed toilet, or even a community centre. Either way, your contribution will go towards helping and changing people's lives. Raleigh International supports this by stating that "as a volunteer you will be helping to improve the quality of life and provide sustainable valuable resources."

Project management and logistics coordination

Katie Aston joined Raleigh's spring expedition in Costa Rica as a logistics coordinator and project manager. Katie felt that a Raleigh expedition might be a way to regain confidence in the workplace, allow her to live and work in Latin America, and equip her with new skills. Raleigh was her only consideration, as she knew of its reputation.

As a project manager she was responsible for the welfare, happiness, safety, and personal development of a group of 17-–24-year-olds. In her role as logistics coordinator she was in charge of designing suitable menus, placing orders with the wholesaler, and allocating food to the groups, working within a tight budget. As a member of the field-base staff, she was also required to assist other members of staff and operate the radio.

On reflection, Katie acknowledges that her experience on the Raleigh expedition gave her the confidence that she can be thrown into a variety of situations and cope well outside her comfort zone. She previously felt uncomfortable speaking in front of a group and was overly concerned about how she came across to people. In completing the trek she realised she was mentally and physically stronger than she had originally thought. She also realised that she was more positive than she thought and that she was able to lead a group of young people.

After eight years of working for a food production company, Jonathan Keevins decided on a well-earned career break. From his career break he wanted to experience different cultures, visit different countries, and take himself out of his comfort zone, trying new experiences to see how he would cope. He also wanted to devote some time to charity work. Strangely enough, Jonathan met an ex-Raleigh International project manager in a bar in Glasgow. They chatted about her Raleigh experience in Namibia, and after consulting Raleigh's website, Jonathan successfully applied to join an expedition to Costa Rica and Nicaragua as the logistics manager, expedition driver, and project manager.

Jonathan says the logistics team was one of the busiest teams on the expedition and played a crucial role in all aspects of delivering a safe, efficient, and on-budget experience. More specifically, the team was responsible for kit, tools, food, cleaning products, vehicles, communications (i.e., radios and maps), and the maintenance of the field base and the shop. Most aspects of expedition touch logistics in some way, and Jonathan says it's a great role for really getting to know the full expedition and everyone within it. It can be overwhelming at first, but if you take one thing at a time, it is manageable and you'll love it. Skills Jonathan brought to this role included over fifteen years of logistics knowledge and experience, knowing what jobs had to be prioritised in order to run an efficient department, good listening skills, problem solving, being logically minded, and having good numeracy skills.

Jonathan is grateful that his Raleigh experience enabled him to learn so much about himself as a person as well as others.

Where does your money go?

Some people find it surprising that they have to pay to undertake a volunteer project abroad, as, after all, they are giving their time to work on the project. However, volunteer and expedition projects are now very carefully managed, which of course means they cost money to run. i-to-i Volunteer and Adventure Travel, like other volunteer organizations, describe how your volunteer fees are spent.

- Pre-departure support – guidance and advice to prepare you for your trip before you leave the country
- In-country support – local staff who are dedicated to making sure you have all the support you need while you're away
- Airport pick-up – you will be collected and taken to your destination
- Cultural orientation – you'll be given a useful talk about local customs, the surrounding area and how to get the most from your experience
- Emergency support – an emergency support line is provided if the situation is required

Source: http://www.i-to-i.com/about-i2i/money-goes/

i-to-i Volunteer and Adventure Travel also state that typically 52 percent (and often more) of your fee goes straight back into the local economy, covering accommodation expenses, meals, local transportation, and supporting the local wages. By paying your way, you are "adding value to the cause rather than adding to the project's cost" (http://www.i-to-i.com/docs/volunteer/ventures_uk.pdf).

Raleigh International explain the expense behind their three-month expeditions: "Money from venturers covers the cost of running our permanent field bases and the costs of having permanent staff – without this infrastructure we simply could not build up the relationships we have with the communities and project partners to create sustainable projects" (http://www.raleighinternational.org/files/Where%20does%20your%20money%20go.pdf). According to Gap Year for Grown Ups, costs vary across volunteer projects, but your fee covers your living expenses, a project donation, and managing and developing the Gap Year for Grown Ups business (http://www.gapyearforgrownups.co.uk/Ten-Reasons-to-Volunteer).

Rosie Pebble recalls she paid just under £3,000 for her three-month project and says that while this may sound expensive, when you realise what you receive for your money, it really isn't. Whilst she paid for her own flight, Projects Abroad arranged her travel insurance, a host family for her to live with who provided all meals, and a work placement that suited her, and they dealt with all the legal child protection issues and arranged her permits (the rules are very strict in Romania). They also met her at the airport and settled her in with her host family, showed her around the city, organised social evenings, and supplied her with bus passes to get to work and a mobile phone. What should not be underestimated is the cost of "peace of mind." If you've never volunteered before, then sourcing your experience through an established organisation will give you a certain level of comfort in knowing that your personalised needs are being considered and that you'll be looked after during your placement.

What sort of accommodation can you expect during a volunteer project?

As a volunteer, the type of accommodation available to you may vary depending on the country or village in which you undertake your project. Here are some of the accommodation types:

Homestay

If you choose a homestay, you would live with a local family sometimes referred to as a "host" family. Cultural exchanges will be offered in the form of language, cooking, customs, and beliefs. This is a fantastic way to truly experience another culture.

On-site accommodation

This type of accommodation varies depending on location. It could be in the form of tents, huts, or dorms.

Guesthouse or hotel

Generally locally owned, guesthouses and hotels are a great way to meet other travellers.

Volunteer house

A volunteer house is a great place to meet fellow travellers who are working on the same project as you. If you volunteer with Mad Adventurer (www.madventurer.com), you'll stay in a communal "Mad House," which provides a basic level of comfort, complete with a local cook to ensure you take full advantage of experiencing the local cuisine.

Is volunteering right for you?

There are lots of options available to you, and selecting a project may prove challenging, as they are all such worthwhile and important causes. After reading the descriptions above, you may be feeling a strong preference towards one or two. Quite a few of these organisations offer "open days" where you can meet the staff and people who've previously undertaken the projects, plus learn more about the projects on offer. It's a great way to make a more informed decision.

I've attended a couple and found them very useful, especially hearing the stories from the volunteers themselves, who provide a balanced view of the projects they were involved in, in order to give you a realistic insight into what would be expected of you and what you could gain from the experience. They may also share with you things they really missed from home, such as a nice cup of tea. One volunteer mentioned that during his project he slept in a hammock and found that when he returned home he found it difficult to adapt to sleeping in a bed again. He spent his first night back home in London in his hammock in the back garden!

To sum up, "whatever you do, it's important to remember that the purpose of volunteering is helping others. The life of a volunteer brings up many unexpected challenges, and volunteers are expected to work long hours in basic conditions. Put simply, volunteering is hard work. On the other hand, if you rise to the challenge, you may just find that volunteering is the most rewarding experience of your life" (Bindloss "Volunteering").

Knowing what you know now about volunteer projects, use the space below to answer the questions.

Write down volunteer projects that appeal to you.

_____

_____

_____

What would you like to achieve by participating in a project?

_____

_____

_____

Are there any skills, characteristics, or abilities you would like to develop whilst working on a volunteer project?

_____

_____

_____

If you are thinking seriously about participating in a volunteer project, list three action points you would be willing to take forward immediately. (For example, attend an open day, speak to someone who has completed a volunteer project abroad, or do some research on the internet to find out more information).

1. _____

2. _____

3. _____

Paid Work

One way of funding your career break, or a means of extending it, is to work while you are away. Bindloss ("Working") notes "this means you can travel for longer and further – and achieve more of your goals." There are many options to earning money whilst you're away, some of which have been identified below:

Buying and running your own business

In 2001, Allan Hobart, from London (though currently living in New York) took his first nine-month sabbatical and travelled through Thailand, Australia and New Zealand. He really enjoyed the experience and wanted to explore more of the world so took a 3-year career break in 2005, at the age of 33, with a friend who he had met during his sabbatical.

They started in Venezuela and travelled through South America for 6-months before travelling up through Central America for 6-weeks, arriving in Guatemala. Up until Guatemala, the whole trip was about sightseeing and experiencing the cultures of the various countries and learning a little Spanish. They initially went to San Pedro La Laguna, Guatemala, to live with local families and study Spanish but also to volunteer after Hurricane Stan had destroyed nearby villages. Once there, they enjoyed the village and the people so much they decided to extend their stay and found work at local bars owned by expatriates to help provide funding for their continued stay and onward travel.

As a volunteer, Allan helped out in a school, teaching English to children orphaned by the hurricane and also helped build temporary shelters for families who lost their homes. After 3-months in San Pedro meeting many wonderful friends and a girlfriend (now his wife), they needed to leave to finish the rest of their round the world ticket but Allan planned to come back to Guatemala to meet up with his girlfriend and look to buy a business, either in Guatemala or somewhere else in Central America.

Allan and his friend went to Mexico before backpacking through Southeast Asia with a short stay in Sydney. While he was travelling, an opportunity arose for his girlfriend to buy the bar and restaurant she was managing at the time so she contacted Allan and they decided to buy it. After finishing his trip and a brief stay back in the UK, Allan moved to San Pedro and he and his girlfriend started their new business venture together which they ran for two years. Allan learned the 'ins and outs' of running a small business whilst improving his Spanish as well as developing the patience to accept a culture/lifestyle that doesn't operate as fast as the first world. He also claims "he became a heck of a bartender." His business was very successful which allowed them to lead a comfortable lifestyle in Guatemala. Although what they took home each week was much less, however, this was all relative because of the inexpensive cost of living.

While running an enjoyable and successful business, Allan and his girlfriend continued to actively support the community by hosting numerous charity events at the bar to benefit local schools and other community projects. As football (soccer) was, and still is, Allan's passion, whilst playing on a local team, he also coached children and managed a youth team in the local league. As a qualified referee, he volunteered his time to train the PE teachers the correct rules of the game so as to improve the standard of the refereeing.

Prior to his career break Allan worked as a Project Manager on Business Transformation projects and returned to work for the same company in February 2008, however, this time within the Financial

Crime department, leading various projects Having returned to his career, Allan and his now wife still continue to contribute funding to these organizations.

Reflecting on his career break, Allan notes "The highs were learning about the many cultures around the world, meeting some great people and seeing some amazing sights. Another high was running a successful business which we sold for double what we bought it for and were ranked as the top bar and restaurant in travel guides (Lonely Planet) when previously the business wasn't mentioned. The amazing experience taught me about life outside of the first world and really helped me appreciate how fortunate we are. It was an amazing experience that will stay with me for life. The experience helped me de-stress from the quick pace of my everyday banking life." Allan's top advice for anyone thinking about taking a career break is "DO IT!!! Never fear what you haven't experienced and seek out the things you enjoy."

Teaching English

Teaching English has become extremely popular for people who wish to experience living in another country and experience a different culture whilst working to support themselves. Teaching English as a Foreign Language, more commonly known as TEFL, is a qualification that can be studied through open learning or in a classroom environment. Depending on the course provider, the courses may vary in length and difficulty. Schools abroad have become more particular in whom they allow to teach in their schools. As the TEFL qualification has become so popular, schools are in a position to be more selective. TEFL providers generally assist students in obtaining roles abroad; however, it's a much more formal process than you would expect.

Ann Sullivan, completed a TEFL course and spent one year in Bangkok, Thailand, teaching English to high school students. Ann was surprised by the amount of work required to complete the qualification, not to mention the essays and assignments she had to complete in order to pass. She was also surprised to learn that her school required her to wear a uniform; on hearing the description, a combination of grey and peach, it sounded more like an eighties bridesmaid's dress than a teacher's uniform! Ann was under the impression that teaching English abroad would be quite an easy task and so didn't appreciate just how much work was involved when she arrived and started her assignment. She recently said, "I didn't realize there would be so much work involved and all the class planning and preparation. My dream of marking papers on the beach is now a distant fantasy."

Teaching English abroad may sound like a great idea to earn money whilst experiencing living in another country, but before embarking on your studies, consider the following:

- *Security of the country* – is the country a safe one in which to live and work?
- *Living conditions* – will you be living with a local family, in an apartment or sharing with other teachers?
- *Support* – is there an organisation providing the necessary support? What would happen in the case of an emergency?
- *Location* – will you be based in a remote village or a town? Will you have access to a town, phone, internet, laundry services, etc.?
- *Cost* – will you be required to cover any costs, and if so, what are they?
- *Flight* – is your placement provider covering the cost of your flight, or are you responsible for it?
- *Visa* – who is covering the cost, and who makes the application?
- *Length of time* – how long do you plan on teaching abroad?
- *Legalities* - will you have to sign a contract?
- *Your responsibilities* – has your employer provided you with a "job description" detailing the duties and responsibilities of the role?
- *Transport* – are you being collected from the airport on arrival? Will you have your own car, or is local transport available for you to get around?

- *Compensation/pay* – how much will you be paid? Will it be enough to cover your expenses?
- *Other teachers* – with whom will you be working?
- *Local amenities* – are there shops close enough to the school where you'll be living to buy your daily and weekly essentials?

Jon Stewart moved to Granada, Spain, to take up a job teaching English. He didn't have any qualifications but was lucky, as the school didn't require any. He firstly inherited some classes from a friend at a small school on the outskirts of town, then gained some more himself by going around some language schools during pre-term. Jon says that his year was filled with screaming children, complaining parents, and clocks running so slowly that Picasso could have drawn them himself. Whilst the kids behaved badly, as they didn't really want to be at school, Jon managed to find the right balance between discipline and fun. It then became more of a pleasure to teach them, and he felt genuinely sad to leave them at the end of the year, when his classes had finished.

Jon admits he's not a natural performer, so having to spend all day presenting and teaching was very draining. He also acknowledged that he didn't particularly enjoy teaching, but the year he spent in Granada was one of the happiest he's ever experienced.

If you're thinking of undertaking a TEFL course, then you may wish to do some research, speak to people who've completed the course, and returned from teaching assignments abroad. This way you'll be in a position to make a more informed decision before making any commitments. To assist you in your research, listed below are a few TEFL providers.

- **TEFL** – www.tefl.com
- **Dave's ESL Café** – www.eslcafe.com
- **i-to-I Volunteer and Travel Abroad** – www.i-to-i.com/tefl
- **TEFL Net** – www.tefl.net
- **ihBangkok** – www.ihbangkok.com

- **International Teacher Training Organisation** – www.teflcertificatecourses.com/specials
- **TEFL courses offered in Australia** – www.teflcertificationabroad.com/search/australia

Freelancing your skills

Freelancing could be an option for you, depending on your career type and skills. Bindloss ("Working") notes "many freelancers deal with their clients over the web, so you could theoretically work from anywhere with an electric socket and a phone line". If you are likely to freelance while away, Bindloss advises that you build up a list of clients before you go. If you feel you have a skill that can be utilised on a freelance basis, then visit the following websites.

1) *Elance* (www.elance.com) allows you to bid for projects in your area of expertise, such as web developing, designing, writing, programming, and so much more. Review the posted jobs and bid for your work. If you win, simply negotiate your terms and conditions directly with your employer, and you're on your way.

2) *Peopleperhour* (www.peopleperhour.com) allows small businesses to hire top talent remotely for small projects or a few hours a week, which could easily be integrated into your travels. Launching in 2008, peopleperhour have outsourced over £22,100,000 worth of services across the word to small and medium-sized businesses.

3) *oDesk* (www.odesk.com) "hire, manage and pay a distributed work team as if everyone were in your office." Like other freelance websites, they are changing how the world works by offering a complete working solution online. Since its inception in 2004, it has doubled in size each year. All you need to do is post your profile, apply for jobs, and interview for free.

4) *Weedle*, an application you can find through Facebook, is another resource where you can promote your skills so that people who are looking for your type of service can locate you. To get started, simply create a profile, add your skills, upload a photo, and start contacting people, to advertise your services.

You may even like the article "Freelance Writing Advice - How to Make Money While You Travel the World as Freelance Writer" (ezinearticles. com/?Freelance-Writing-Advice---How-to-Make-Money-While-You-Travel-the-World-As-Freelance-Writer&id=4415203) by Yuwanda Black, a freelance writer since 1993, who took her freelance writing career on the road in 2010. Read Yuwanda's story and note her hints and tips on setting up your own freelance writing business.

I was somewhat jealous when I came across the website Have Internet Will Travel (www.haveinternetwilltravel.com). In a nutshell, in September 2008 Mike Schimanowsky and Kelly Hale, veteran web designers, both at the age of twenty-eight, sold their worldly belongings for a life of nomadic freelancing and travel after ten years working in the internet industry. Sound scary? Or does it sound exciting?

Mike and Kelly agreed to be interviewed about their real-life experience of what it's like to travel and freelance.

Q - How hard/emotional was it leaving your friends and family behind?

Mike: I was very caught up in the excitement of the moment. There was still so much to do and plan. And so many people to see before we left! Looking back at it all now, it's a blur. We had a few big get-togethers to say good-bye to everyone. I think when we started we were envisioning it to be a year or so of travelling, so there wasn't any permanence in the good-byes at the time. Almost three years later, we now go home to visit about once a year for a few weeks at a time. I think the hardest things for us are Christmas, the weddings we can't attend, and the new babies and kids running around that we hardly know.

Kelly: I hate to say that it really wasn't that hard at all, but, well, that's the truth. We had been planning for so long, I was just ready to go, caught up in the excitement of everything and eager to begin this new chapter of our life. It wasn't till much, much later that I began to realize just how much I missed my family and friends, and still do all the time. My brother has had two kids since we've left, and several friends have gotten married. It's hard to be away for important events, but when we do get to visit, we slip right back into the swing of things as if we haven't been gone at all.

Q - What specifically did you do for a career prior to leaving?

Mike: Following the dotcom bomb, I was the technical lead for a design firm for seven years. Web development/nerd stuff.

Kelly: From 1999 to 2002 I worked for a couple of interactive agencies in Vancouver as a web designer. In 2002 I moved to Amsterdam with one of those companies and ended up working for them, as well as another local design company, for the next year or so. Following a bit of travelling I went back to Vancouver and began freelancing for a couple of months before accepting an art director position in the interactive division of an ad agency, where I worked right up till we left.

Q - What led you to the decision to move abroad and become freelancers?

Mike: I was unsatisfied with my work scenario and unmotivated. My career momentum had stagnated and was lacking real challenges. I had worked myself into a situation where I was overseeing and spec'ing projects instead of building them hands-on. I had already started considering going freelance full-time again. In March of 2006 Kelly and I took a month off and travelled to Brazil. It awoke a deep need to see more of the world beyond the usual two-week trip to a resort once or twice a year, and it proved we travel well together. We began asking ourselves how and if we could turn that type of experience into a lifestyle option.

Kelly: I spent a couple of years previously living overseas, and when I returned to Vancouver, I thought it was just a temporary thing. I'd planned to stay no more than a year – just enough time to save some money and plan the next trip, but somehow life got in the way. I fell back in with familiar friends, landed a great job, and before I knew it I was settled. I met Mike and things were going great. The longer I stayed, the harder it became to leave. Almost five years after being back in Vancouver, I started to get the itch again. I realized I was living my life for the weekends and counting my vacation days. Around that time Mike and

I spent a month in Brazil, which I think is what sparked the urge. It started popping up in conversations between us – the "what ifs" and "wouldn't it be great tos"– the more we talked about it the more the possibility turned into reality.

Q - *Had you both had freelance experience beforehand? If so, what projects did you get involved in? How many years experience did you have?*

Mike: I had previously freelanced full-time for two years after the dotcom bomb as a contract web/multimedia developer. I then did smaller projects periodically once I took on a full-time job again.

Kelly: I had very little experience freelancing. I had done several jobs on the side while having the safety net of a full-time job, but aside from a couple of months when I first moved back to Vancouver, I had never really supported myself solely from freelancing.

Q - *What research on freelancing did you do prior to leaving, if any?*

Mike: I was already carrying a pretty consistent freelance workload at the time. I had already quit my job six months before we left to confirm it was doable, both in volume and consistency of work.

Kelly: I really hadn't done a lot. I knew from a few friends who were already freelancing that it was doable, and my company was always looking for freelancers, so I knew that there was work out there. I had planned to quit my full-time job a few months before we left in order to pick up a few clients and get into the swing of things, but when I gave notice at work they asked me to stay until we left.

Q - *How easy was the transition in terms of your working and lifestyle?*

Mike: The transition was quite easy from a work standpoint, since I was already freelancing for months before we left. For a while it felt like vacation, but we soon passed through the 'getting settled' window that we had arranged with clients and got back to work, exploring our new surroundings on slow days and weekends.

Kelly: For me the transition was a little slower. At first I had a hard time finding work. I think people weren't really sure of what it is we were trying to do; they thought we were just on vacation for a year and didn't really want to work. I was picking up enough to pay the bills, but it was a while before people realized that this wasn't just a holiday, but a way of life. Once they realized I was serious about picking up work, things started to roll in.

Q - What are the highlights of being a freelancer?

Mike:
- Setting your own hours.
- You can pick what you want to work on.
- The variety of work.
- I have more pride of ownership for my work as a freelancer.
- The ability to be nomadic.

Kelly: I think Mike pretty much summed things up. Setting your own hours and choosing the projects you want, plus we usually have pretty great surroundings in which to work; putting in long days in front of a computer is much more satisfying when you can hear waves crashing on the shore or birds chirping in the background. And ending your day watching the sun set over the water with a beer in your hand sure beats walking home to a dreary apartment in the pouring rain.

Q - What are the challenges of being a freelancer?

Mike:
- Setting your own hours.
- Turning work away is really tough for me. I have a very hard time saying no, since the client is already going out on a limb to hire a nomadic freelancer. I worry I won't see work from that client again in the future if I have to turn a project down.
- Finding reliable internet connectivity everywhere we go. It limits some destinations we'd very much like to visit.

Kelly: Balancing work and play is always difficult, especially when we end up in tropical places or those that have a high volume of tourists. It can be hard when everyone you meet is on vacation and you have to work. Also because of our need for internet we rarely go off the beaten path. We tend to stick to more touristy places and don't always get to see as much of a country as we'd like.

Q - How busy is your workload? How much time do you spend working and playing?

Mike: I've been pretty consistently busy since we started travelling. In the beginning I was actually overloaded, because I had lined up too much work in preparation for the move. It got to a point where Kelly and I weren't finding much quality time or travelling, because we had different work schedules. So when things settled down, we started a 9–5, Monday to Friday rule so we could enjoy evenings and weekends together without work getting in the way. Most weeks, I now try to keep working hours between thirty and forty-five hours a week. We try to book a couple weeks off every few months for a good getaway to somewhere new, like a vacation from our permanent vacation.

Kelly: As Mike mentioned, we're pretty consistent, but it took us a while to get to that point. When we first started out, our schedules were a little all over the place, and we found that we were never doing stuff together because one of us was always working. Now we try to keep a more consistent, Monday–Friday/9–5 schedule so that we can spend our weekends together. It's also helped for our clients to have a consistent schedule so that we're available during work hours or at the least able to get back to them within a couple of hours if needed. Some weeks one of us will be busier than the other, but we usually find something to fill the down time, whether that's working on the blog, editing pictures, or lining up new work.

Q - How much control over your projects/workload do you have? Do you pick and choose what you work on?

Mike: I do pick and choose. But I have a hard time saying no to work.

Kelly: I try to be grateful for everything that comes my way, so I try not to say no, unless I really don't have time.

Q - How do you find work?

Mike: All of my work is through referrals and the contacts I've made over 10+ years in the tech/design industry. I do zero business development, and I'm thankful my skill set is in demand.

Kelly: Like Mike, all of my work is through referrals and industry contacts.

Q - Do you feel you earn enough to support your continued lifestyle?

Mike and Kelly: We make enough and then some for a rainy day. Our travels are purposefully slow, limiting the cost of travelling and maximizing the benefits of being "local." Until our recent relocation to the EU, we've primarily been in countries where the Canadian dollar to local currency has been an advantage. The cost of living is usually less than living in Vancouver, Canada, regardless of where we go.

Q - How often do you get paid when freelancing? How do you negotiate your compensation?

Mike: My long term-clients and I have fairly informal relationships. I estimate projects based on the technical specifications and hours required, and schedule it into my workflow. I'm typically paid at the completion of a job, net thirty. I don't use formal contracts unless requested by a client, though that could bite me back one day. For new clients, I typically ask for 50 percent up front and 50 percent upon completion. Some of my clients have me on payroll, so I get paid every fifteen days by direct deposit based on the hours I submit. I try to keep it fairly flexible for my clients and have family back home handle depositing mailed payments for me, but I manage my invoicing and banking online and use PayPal as well.

Kelly: It varies a bit from client to client, and project to project. Some projects I provide a quote for an entire job, and others I bill hourly. When I freelance with agencies I typically get paid every fifteen days, but for smaller clients usually upon completion of the project. Like Mike, my mom handles deposits of any mailed payments and online banking and PayPal.

Q - Do you feel living abroad whilst freelancing has changed you? If so, how?

Mike: Definitely. Travel changes people. Aside from just being able to experience and appreciate how other people live day-to-day in other parts of the world, I'm addicted to a brand new spectrum of weird snack foods. Also, I'll never be able to go back to working in a cubicle.

Kelly: I think we've definitely changed. It's hard to pinpoint exactly what it is that's different, though. Perhaps the biggest thing is just realizing how much choice we have over our lives. If we don't like where we're living, we can move on; if we don't want to work on a certain project, we can say no. If we're not happy with something, we change it. I think too many people get stuck in this idea of what life is supposed to be like – go to school, get a job, get married, buy a house, have kids, retire. Your life can be whatever you want it to be, and it's the choices you make that define it. People often say, "You're so lucky," but luck has nothing to do with it; we chose this.

Q - What advice would you give someone who is thinking about taking a career break and freelancing to support their experiences?

Mike: It's still a job, though the view is much better from here. When I was previously employed and near ending my employment, my thoughts were to either a) go freelance or b) quit the industry and try something completely new. It took me the first six months of travelling to really shake away the cynicism I had built up around my job and figure out exactly what I needed in my life, but I'm glad I was able to transition it into a position I'm now enjoying and able to utilize those years of connections and relationships to my advantage. A clean break would have been cleaner, but I don't think I could sustain this lifestyle starting from the ground up again.

Kelly: I'd say go for it, but figure out what works for you. There are lots of ways to make a go of things, but what works for some may not work for others. Our work demands are a lot compared to many people trying to live a nomadic life. Finding your own balance between work, travel, and budget is important in figuring how to make this lifestyle work.

Q - At what point (if any) would you decide to move back to Canada? What factors would contribute to a decision to moving back?

Mike :
- Family and friends are a big motivator to go back home. We're missing out on the early years of some of our family members. Missing weddings and birthdays. And we miss the ease of familiar faces sometimes.
- There are no good paved motorcycle roads in SE Asia, except for Malaysia.
- If global warming gives Canada a tropical climate.
- If the work dried up due to economical reasons.

Kelly: Family and friends definitely, but other than that, I'm not really sure. These days we have a hard time deciding where we want to go next month. Canada's not really on our radar right now.

Q - Any other comments?

Mike – You'll never know what could have been if you don't jump in.

Kelly - There's only so much planning and research you can do. At some point you just need to do it.

How inspiring is their story? I strongly recommend you read Mike and Kelly's blog (http://haveinternetwilltravel.com), where you can read more on their experiences of living and working overseas, together with a host of other useful information, such as budgeting and planning.

If the lifestyle enjoyed by Mike and Kelly sounds right for you, visit the following sites to learn how to set yourself up as a freelancer.

- **Gotham Writers Workshop (New York)** –nytkn.writing classes.com/Partner/GenrePage.php?ClassGenreCode =HF&PartnerID=NYT&gclid=CPvzsMax3acCFYFB4Qod9GA W8A
- **Online Business** – onlinebusiness.about.com/lr/ freelancers/289170/2
- **Life of the Freelancer** – lifeofthefreelancer.com
- **I freelance, Freelance jobs and professionals** –www. ifreelance.com/landing.aspx?ag=580&k=31443&mt=p&gclid =CM2K3qSz3acCFYob4QodeU9G9w
- **Freelance University** –www.freelanceuniversity.com
- **Freelance Writing** –www.chrisblogging.com

Working in Tourism and Hospitality

The travel and tourism industry is a huge employer, employing a staggering 72 million people worldwide. The seasonal nature of the work may perfectly suit someone taking a gap year, although, on the whole, the work is hard and the pay low (Griffiths, 2008). In my experience people typically don't take a career break to earn lots of money; it's more about the experience than the pay packet.

Working in a bar

Can you pull a pint? Create the perfect cocktail? Make small talk with the punters? Bar and hospitality work are probably the most common form of work for travellers, as little or no experience is usually required. Generally, in tourist destinations the turnover of employees is very high, as travellers form the majority of their staff. Depending on the country, if you're looking for bar work, the best and most effective option is to cold call, that is, walk in off the street and ask the manager if they're looking for any full-time or part-time workers. Have your CV ready to hand over and be prepared to discuss why you should be considered for the job. Other options are to ask the locals if they know of any jobs and visit the local supermarkets, as they may have job postings in their windows.

Working in resorts

Working in resorts is a great way to spend quality time in another country, meet other travellers and tourists, and earn some money to support your future travels. Most holiday resorts hire extra staff for the tourist season, so these can be fantastic places to pick up short-term work. With a valid work permit or working holiday visa, you could find work in hotels, restaurants, shops, and bars (Bindloss "Working").

According to Susan Griffiths (2008:195), "it's not at all unusual for people who have been working in business or industry for a few years to want to work in the sun for a while and by targeting the right resorts and the right companies, you can find something suitable for a grown-up gap year." However, it's not just the sun that attracts career breakers to resorts.

Kelly Taylor and her husband, for better or for worse, work together at the same training company in London. They took a sabbatical from their jobs to embark on an experience they had been dreaming about for quite some time. In the Q&A below, Kelly shares their story.

What inspired/motivated you to take a career break?
I went straight from university to work in the city with no gap year or stint travelling. Whilst this never really bothered me, as the years passed I began to feel a twinge of regret that I had never taken time out. Still, I really don't know if I ever would have gotten around to seriously considering a career break if it were not for a completely unplanned set of personal circumstances.

Having been through a couple of difficult years (from a family perspective), we both felt burnt out and pretty confident that too much time in life is wasted doing what you feel you *should* do, not necessarily what you *want* to do. We both felt very strongly that life is not for wasting, and that there must be a way to maintain our careers and associated responsibilities whilst opening ourselves up to a different way of living.

I don't think any of this was a conscious process, and I think we had decided to take the career break before stopping to consider what had led us to the decision.

I think it was a collision of personal circumstances, love of a particular pastime, a few glasses of wine, and some supportive friends that provided the motivation. Plus, I happened to meet a friendly career break coach who was more than happy to pour fuel on the fire by providing lots of helpful advice and encouragement.

How did you approach it with your employer?
We just asked! We weren't sure how it would be received, as we both work for the same firm, and to my knowledge we were the first people to broach the subject of a career break. Fortunately, they were fully appraised of the family situation we had been in and were supportive of us using the career break to prevent burnout and help maintain levels of performance at work. We were also lucky in that the period of time we wanted to take for our career break coincides with the off-season in our industry. We made sure they understood we had considered the needs of the business in planning the break.

How long is your break?
Five months, December 2012–April 2013

What will you be doing on your break, and why did you choose to do it?
We'll be working! We are going to work as chalet hosts in the French Alps. Looking after up to fourteen new guests every week, we'll be doing everything from cleaning rooms, to making cakes, to cooking three-course dinners six days per week.

Why did we choose this? Well, a combination of factors. I suppose there is the fact that we love France and holiday there at least twice a year. We also love skiing and enjoy being in the mountain environment.

We were attracted to the chalet host position specifically because not only are your living expenses part of the package (so our career break is not eating into savings/putting us into debt), but the role is also very people-focussed, and we hope the skills we have gained in corporate life will be hugely transferable to providing a first-class customer experience to our guests. Our career break isn't about escaping from work; it's about experiencing work in a different context – different challenges, different demands, different rewards.

Oh, and we get to ski five days a week too.

How do you think your experience will change you?
As well as learning new skills, and new ways to apply existing ones, my personal hope is that it will help me gain perspective on where I want to go from here – personally and professionally. Perhaps I'll return to my current role, refreshed, revived and with a toolkit of new skills at my disposal? Perhaps I'll decide that in the long term I'd like to change industries, countries, or perhaps work for myself? Also, there is the small issue of starting a family at some point over the next five to eight years; what else do I want to achieve before taking this step?

What are your fears/concerns, if any?
Failure, injury, marriage meltdown, problems with tenants – you name it! Seriously, the list of potential things that you could worry about are endless, so you need to be quite pragmatic, I think. On a personal level, I do occasionally worry that I won't provide the quality of experience that I hope to be able to provide, and about how well my husband and I will work in such close quarters. On a more practical level, my biggest concerns are getting seriously ill/ injured. This is not just hypochondria - it would potentially mean my chalet host contract would be terminated if I couldn't work).

How did you manage your property back in London?
We own a flat in South London that we let to tenants about six weeks before we are due to leave and are living with my sister-in-law until then. As we had to let the flat for twelve months, we will have to find someone different to rent when we return in April. We rented quite a bit in the last few years, so we're relatively relaxed about the prospect of retuning without anywhere to live! Our family are really supportive and have many spare rooms!

How does taking a career break make you feel?
Excited, concerned, lucky, anxious, relieved, overwhelmed, brave, happy, nervous, free – the lot, really. Mostly I still feel like it's not really happening, despite the fact I've only two weeks left of work, and that I'm living in my sister-in-law's spare room, and that my flat is rented to strangers, and that all my belongings are in storage, etc. I'm not really sure at what point it's going to kick in that it's really happening – I'll let you know!

What do your friends and family think?
I think they all went through stages – disbelief, cynicism, then intrigued, supportive, positive, and now some of them are downright excited! I was surprised at the amount of poorly disguised jealousy - certain friends continue to take the "It's all right for some" or "I wish I could just carelessly abandon my responsibilities and take off for five months" approach. The implication being that what we are doing is stupid and irresponsible.

Funnily enough, the person who has been most positive and supportive throughout is my husband's sixteen-year-old son. Despite not seeing us for five months, he's taken responsibility for ensuring all family members are webcam-enabled so we can all catch up via Skype, etc. He hopes to do a ski season during his gap year.

What are your expectations on your return?
That's kind of the exciting part – I really don't know. Practically, we're a pretty adaptable couple and aren't really fazed by the idea of returning home in late April and having to find somewhere to live and retrieve all of our stuff from storage, all before starting work again on the first of May. Beyond that – how we will feel, how we will have changed as people, in outlook – it's all still to be written.

And anything else you wish to include?
I can't think of anything, and my typing fingers hurt.

Sports instructing

This type of work is not suitable for everyone, as you will need a certain level of fitness and an interest and ability in the chosen sport. You're also likely to need an internationally recognised instructor qualification. Bindloss ("Working") believes that skiing is the easiest adventure industry to work in and that the scuba diving industry is also well set up for career breakers. He suggests the following companies to source work for skiing instructor work:

- **Mark Warner** – www.markwarner-recruitment.co.uk
- **Specialist Holiday Group** – www.shgjobs.co.uk
- **SkiStaff** – www.skistaff.co.uk

Labouring or working on a farm

Do you like the idea of getting your hands dirty on a construction site, getting up at the crack of dawn to milk cows, or picking fruit? To find a construction job, Bindloss ("Working") suggests visiting construction sites and speaking to the foreman or contacting employment agencies that specialise in construction jobs. As for farm work, plenty of travellers pay their way by picking fruit and working on farms. Bindloss claims that Australia is a well-organised location for this and that farm jobs are often advertised in local job centres.

Cruising through your career break

Cruise ships are a great way to earn money while you travel. You need relevant experience, and most jobs are arranged through specialist agencies. However, make sure you have your "sea legs," as you may experience motion sickness, which wouldn't be fun if you were stuck on a ship in the middle of the ocean with no land in sight. It's important to be prepared with regard to your living conditions, as you may have to share a cabin with other workers with limited space and a very small bathroom. But I hear the regular staff parties are a blast.

Tour leader

As the name suggests, a tour leader travels with groups of tourists to each location; this a great way to combine work and travel. However, this tends to be an option for only highly organised people with years of travel experience (Bindloss "Working"). Remember, there are many pros and cons to being a tour leader, and it's not suitable for everyone, as we discovered earlier with the guide whom Ronan met during his South American travels. Here a few pros and cons to consider.

Pros	Cons
• Travel around the world	• Never in the same place for very long
• Become an expert in your region	• Travel can be repetitive, as you're visiting the same places over and over again
• Meet lots of new people	• New friendships are very short-lived
• Exposure to lots of different countries and cultures	• No home, as constantly on the move
• Living out of a backpack	• Living out of a backpack
• Learning new skills	• Are your new skills transferable?
• Providing information to people on a new country, culture, and customs	• People sometimes don't listen to what you say or are not very interested
• Learn more about the style of other travellers	• People bug you with the smallest of problems, complain and moan about transport, accommodation, and other travellers
• The travel company will cover your transportation and accommodation costs during your trip	• Don't get paid a lot of money, and you can't rely on tips
• Always surrounded by people	• Limited personal time
• Not a 9–5 job	• Long hours

• Freedom to wear what you like	• Wearing the same clothes over and over, as have to carry personal belongings

Seen Suwamin, from Bangkok, Thailand, has been a tour leader for over five years, covering all regions across Thailand, and he has worked for some well-known travel companies, including Gap Adventures, Nutty's Adventures, and Grasshopper. When asked about the advantages of his job, he stated that "meeting new people, the freedom of travelling, and of course the tips from travellers at the end" made his job more enjoyable. On the down side, however, what he dislikes the most about being a tour leader is "rude people." Seen doesn't mind being away from home on a regular basis, as his job sometimes demands that he's away for two weeks every month. He says that being a tour guide never feels like working when he is *actually* working, plus the pay isn't too bad.

Temping in an office

A great way to earn money whilst adding some experience to your CV, temping is an easy way for anyone with office experience to pick up short-term work with reasonable pay. Temps are generally employed by an agency, so you'll need a work permit that covers you for the kind of work you are doing. You may be able to start your job hunt before you leave home by registering with an international recruitment agency (Bindloss "Working").

To help you in your search, visit *Working Abroad Magazine* (www.workingabroadmagazine.com). Its website offers a host of information on the following working-abroad opportunities.

- Agriculture
- Airline
- Archaeology
- Au pair
- Cruise ships

- Hospitality
- Sailing instructor
- Scuba
- Surfing
- Summer camp
- Tour guiding
- Volunteer – animals and relief work
- Ski
- Yacht

They also provide details of overseas recruiters, including:

- PGL UK – School Trips, Skiing, Camps and More
- Volunteer Teaching Abroad with i-to-i
- AirPro Working Holidays
- Yummy Jobs Work Placements Abroad
- InGlobe Greek Recruitment Agency
- Thomson TUI Travel and Sports Jobs Abroad
- Crown Recruitment for Royal Caribbean Cruise Lines
- Next Step Australia Job Finder Service
- Playaway Tenerife Working Holidays
- GVI – Global Vision International
- Michael Page International Recruitment Consultants

Professional Work

Professional "paid work" may be available only if you have resigned from your current job and are under no contractual obligations, so that you are free to work abroad if you choose. If you're on a sabbatical, it's probably fair to suggest that you may be under certain contractual limitations and may not be able to undertake any form of paid work. It's best to check at the time you make your application to ensure you are clear about what you can and can't do.

For some, undertaking professional work whilst on a career break may not be appealing, as it's supposed to be a "break" from your career, but for others it is a great opportunity to learn some new skills, enhance their CV, and gain experience of working in another country and culture. A good friend of mine was made redundant from her role in banking (after a company merger) and left the UK in 2009. After spending six months travelling, she moved to Brazil and spent eighteen months working in a similar role, though in a different industry. She now speaks fluent Portuguese, has firsthand knowledge and experience of the cultural ways of the local people, and understands the challenges of finding a job (it's all about who you know) and the stresses of setting herself up in an apartment (requiring a guarantor, buying all the electrical goods, having to paint it at the end of her lease). She returned to the UK in late 2010 and enjoyed Christmas with her family before commencing a new role in the new year.

Depending on your personal situation, qualifications, and work history, you may be able to work in a more "professional" capacity during your break. However, this process may be more involved, and it's important to be aware of the facts.

Sponsorship

There are many rules and regulations surrounding who is eligible to receive sponsorship to work in another country, and you may have to meet certain criteria. If you just turn up in a foreign country expecting to work legally, you may find yourself disappointed and unemployed. To avoid this, source a job before you leave home, so that when you arrive in your chosen country you have all the legal documentation to hand, plus the security of being employed. How do you find a job? As a starting point, contact the recruitment agencies in the country/city where you wish to work, and they will recommend you for roles if your qualifications, skills, and work history match the roles they hold on their books.

Visa

A visa is a "certificate issued or a stamp marked (on the applicant's passport) by the immigration authorities of a country to indicate that the applicant's credentials have been verified and he or she has been granted permission to enter the country for a temporary stay within a specified period of time. A work visa gives the applicant permission to stay and take up employment, for a specific job and only for a limited time" (BusinessDictionary.com).

Government regulations are becoming tighter as the criteria to apply for visas are more stringent than ever before, thus making it difficult (but not impossible) to be granted a visa to work abroad, in a professional capacity. For example, banks in Asia are being pressured by the government to hire local talent; hence, opportunities to work in the financial sector in Asia are becoming scarcer, and fewer ex-pats are moving there.

If you wish to apply for a work visa, you may have to fulfil the following criteria.

- You have "extraordinary abilities" in the arts, sciences, education, business, or athletics.
- You are an outstanding professor or researcher.
- You are an executive manager with multinational experience.

Types of visas include:

- Highly Skilled Immigrant visa
- Business visa
- Student visa
- Work permit
- Entrepreneur visa
- Worker registration scheme
- Investor visa

To find out more information regarding visas in your country of interest, see the following websites.

- **Global Visa** – www.globalvisas.com
- **Work Permit** – www.workpermit.com
- **Australia, Canada, America, and the UK** – www.migrationexpert.com
- **Hong Kong** – www.immd.gov.hk/ehtml/hkvisas_4.htm
- **Singapore** – www.mfa.gov.sg
- **South Africa** – www.home-affairs.gov.za/Service%20 Centers.html
- **Mexico** – www.mexperience.com/living/immigration-mexico.php
- **UK** – www.ukvisaandimmigration.co.uk
- **Brazil** – www.brazilsf.org/visa_work_eng.htm
- **New Zealand** – www.visabureau.com/newzealand/new-zealand-visa

Vicky Gardner moved from Birmingham, UK, to Melbourne, Australia, along with her parents when she was twenty-three, giving up her career to focus more on her family following the sudden death of her younger brother. Given the circumstances of her move, Vicky did find the upheaval extremely difficult and at times questioned her decision to leave her job to accompany her parents to Australia. However, over time she grew to enjoy life in Melbourne. Like many cities overseas, Melbourne has a huge network of ex-pats, which can be invaluable in helping people to relocate and familiarise themselves in their new surroundings. There is often a great support system within corporate entities for families relocating, and many international cities now have myriad services to assist with the transition too.

Vicky also had something of a rocky ride with regard to the terms of her visa and its associated working rights. Having secured a temporary resident visa, she worked in sales for some time before rejoining the hospitality industry, in which she had been employed back in the UK. This was partly on the advice of the immigration lawyers that Vicky had engaged to assist her as her visa's term drew to a close; they felt that hospitality was one of the favoured industries on the Australian "skills list," which would allow her to secure longer-term working rights. However, having struggled to find an employer who was willing to dedicate the time and money required to sponsor her visa application, she came within two weeks of having to return to the UK when she finally secured a position and sponsorship from a large restaurant chain. Eventually, after six and a half years in the country, and with the support of her new employer, Vicky secured permanent residency ("PR") in 2004.

Over the course of these years, between lawyer's fees, flying in and out of the country, accommodation overseas whilst waiting for new visas, and studying for courses to assist with her PR application, Vicky believes she spent between AUD$20,000 and 30,000. She says if you are thinking of starting life over in a new country, make sure you have researched *all* the possibilities and have plenty of savings in case it all goes horribly wrong! Have a contingency plan and an account with savings to cover the costs.

Sourcing accommodation

Relocating to another country and city costs money. As a professional worker, you will need to find somewhere a bit more permanent to live; therefore, you may need to pay a deposit, rent, and bills. If you need to sign a lease agreement, as we saw with my friend in Brazil, it might be a challenge for the agent to obtain references, given that you're in a foreign country. Depending on how long you wish to work, it might be worthwhile renting a room from someone, as this could keep the costs down and paperwork to a minimum.

Tax

There will be varying laws on taxation in different countries, and I would advise that you check with the local tax office regarding your responsibilities and also see if your home country has a reciprocal arrangement, as you may be able to add your earnings to what you earned in the last tax year of your home country. You may also have to contribute to a health scheme such as Medicare in Australia, National Insurance in the UK, or Social Security in the USA.

Clothes

If your job requires you to dress in a certain way, you may have to spend some of your savings on buying appropriate clothes. If you are working in a professional environment, it might not look so favourable if you turn up in your well-worn travel clothes.

Unpaid Work Experience

Working for free may not appeal to you; however, it may be a great opportunity to add some skills, knowledge, and experience to your tool kit. Your experiences may provide interesting talking points during interviews when you return home, or with your friends and family. It's not every day you get the opportunity to work on a coffee plantation in Kenya, be an assistant editor on a local newspaper in Mexico, or be an au pair in France. It really does depend on what type of experience you're looking for; however, remember this may provide you with a unique experience that will stay with you forever.

If you need some help finding unpaid work experience, then visit the sites below.

- **Work UK** – www.workuk.co.uk
- **Work Experience UK** – www.workexperienceuk.com
- **Indeed** – www.indeed.co.uk

List any unpaid work experience opportunities that appeal to you.

_____

_____

_____

Studying

Learning a new skill or language

Learning a new skill or language during your career break can be an ideal way to boost your CV, change your career, and, of course, have fun at the same time. Think about being able to order your favourite wine in French in a restaurant in France, or tangoing the night away in a salsa class, or working your hands through dough as you make pasta with Paolo, your Italian cooking teacher, or attending a creative writing class to start your own novel.

The type of course you're considering will determine the length and required participation. For example, cooking courses may run between six and ten weeks, whereas language classes may have different levels such as beginner, intermediate, and advanced, and may run concurrently for over three months.

It's also important to consider how you plan to integrate learning a new skill or language into your career break in terms of time, selecting the country in which you wish to undertake the course, and how much the course will cost. For example, you may want to learn Italian in a language school in Florence, which may mean living in Florence for an extended period of time. If becoming fluent is your goal, this could take a few months, which suggests taking a career break that allows you the time to complete this, not to mention ensuring you have the funds to cover your daily living expenses, which would include accommodation, food, utility bills, entertainment costs, books and study materials, and so much more.

Some courses, such as a writing course in Thailand, London, or New York, may take only one week, which makes it easy to slot into your career break. Runa Sadarangani, age thirty-four, from London, enjoyed her day-to-day life but found herself growing restless and felt a need to feed her passion for creativity. Considering her options, Runa started a part-time graphic design course whilst still working full-time. While the decision to work and study at the same time was a practical one, Runa quickly realised that graphic design was *not* the creative expression she thought she was born to do. However, the course highlighted her true passion – the written word.

Disappointed but not discouraged, Runa submerged herself in the daily life of work and trying to meet impossible deadlines. Six months later, Runa heard about a writing course in New York, designed for people who were thinking about writing a book, and covering all the practical issues, such as discovering a niche market and sourcing an agent, as well as the creative issues, such as determining a writing style. She subsequently resigned from her job, booked the course, and jetted off to New York to fulfil her dream. When Runa returned to London, she felt comfortable in the knowledge that she understood the "framework" for writing a book, so that when she chose to start the creative process she understood the methodology.

During my first career break, I headed to LA to train to become a professional photographer. Photography had always been a passion of mine, and I was often complimented on my photography skills and abilities and the photos themselves. Prior to heading to LA, I completed a few photography courses to refresh my skills and learn some new techniques. These courses only heightened my interest, and I was convinced that I would be a great professional photographer and make a living from the industry. I had the passion, drive, technical skills, and was about to embark on learning the "business side".

So, during my time in LA, I experienced the business side of the industry, and I have to admit I wasn't comfortable with what I saw: the expense of all the equipment, and photo shoots being cancelled with minimal notice (with no compensation), not to mention never knowing when you were going to get paid (even though the terms and conditions of payment would be on your invoice). It also made me think how the photography profession didn't fit with my work values, as I valued financial security, commitment, and professionalism. I felt this industry was too volatile for me, and that I would find myself constantly frustrated.

Taking the opportunity to live a "realistic job preview" helped me make an informed decision – becoming a professional photographer was not for me. I'm pleased I had the opportunity to experience the profession hands-on before making a financial and emotional commitment. I can only imagine, if I had jumped straight in, what the consequences would have been. It would be fair to say the experience would not have been positive, and that it would be a decision I would have regretted. Whilst this didn't work out for me, I was happy to retain photography as a hobby and share my photos with family and friends on Facebook.

Like myself and Runa, you might plan your course before you leave, or you may like to leave it until you arrive in a specific country and take advantage of what appeals to you at the time and what's available. To find a course, the most obvious places to start include notice boards at the local shops, asking the locals, or visiting local community centres. Or, if you'd rather be more prepared, then do your research before you leave. Here are some sites to get you started.

- **Abroad Languages** – www.abroadlanguages.com/learn/italian
- **ESL Language Studies Abroad** – www.esl-languages.com
- **The Open University, London** – www.open.ac.uk/openlearn
- **Gap Year for Grown Ups** – www.gapyearforgrownups.co.uk/Learn-New-Skills
- **Real Gap Experiences** – www.realgap.com
- **Anne Aylor Creative Writing Courses** – www.anneaylor.co.uk/WritingCourses.htm
- **Go Learn To** – www.golearnto.com

You may already have some ideas of what you would like to do. If you have, jot them down in the space below.

Ideas of courses you would like to attend.

_____

_____

_____

If you're still weighing whether or not to learn a new skill or language, here are some benefits.

- Meet like-minded people
- Form new friendships and expand your social circle
- Opportunity to try out a new possible career before making a commitment
- Chance to mingle with locals and learn more about another culture
- Discover what values are really important to you
- Find yourself with a possible career change
- Something else to add to your CV
- Opportunity for some fun and adventure
- Discover an interest you wish to continue when you return home
- Chance to step out of your comfort zone

In summary, learning a new language or a skill during your career break can give you so much more than learning the skill itself. The decision as to which course to undertake, how much money to spend, and how much time you have to dedicate to it is a personal one.

Gaining a Professional Qualification.

Gaining a professional qualification during your career break is a great addition to your personal tool kit, not to mention your CV. This could open a few new doors and create opportunities that may not have existed previously.

I hadn't planned on studying during my second career break, but after six weeks of washing dishes and doing laundry for seven people at my sister's house, I began to feel bored, restless, and in need of something more productive, challenging, and stimulating. Given I was used to working in a corporate environment where demands were made of me constantly, spending all my time cleaning up after others wasn't giving me the fulfilment or satisfaction I needed.

During a conversation with my sister over a cup of tea whilst sitting at her dining table, she mentioned I would make a great life coach. I was surprised, as I didn't realise my sister knew what a life coach was. I found this quite intriguing so started to investigate options on the internet. I narrowed down my options to two institutes; however, I was swayed towards the Coaching Institute (www.thecoachinginstitute.com.au) due to the course structure, the personal attention I received in addition to the time frame, cost, and possible career options once the course was complete. The course took one year and cost $5,000 (AUD), and I came away with a "Certificate in Life Coaching."

When I decided to undertake the qualification, I wasn't entirely sure what I wanted from the end result. Did I want to set up my own coaching business? Did I just want to add it to my current credentials? Did I want it just for personal development? All I knew at the time was that it was a topic of interest to me and that it complemented my current skills and experience in recruitment, training, and development, as well as my degree in human resource management, plus other training I had accomplished over the years. My understanding was that I would learn new skills to help people make a difference in their lives, and that it had the potential to separate me from other candidates when interviewing for jobs on my return to London or provide me with a new career.

At the time that seemed enough for me, but, on reflection, I gained so much more. Not only did I learn new skills, knowledge, and a further in-depth understanding of human behaviour, I made many good friends, genuinely helped those I coached, and found it did separate me from others during my job search when I returned to London. In fact, on my CV under the heading "Transferrable Skills," I included "Professional Coach," and this attracted more attention than I had ever anticipated during interviews.

As I am so passionate about the subject, I find myself continuously sharing coaching knowledge and helping people whenever I can. It has truly changed my life. Whilst this has been my experience, it might not suit everyone. Study can take all different forms, and you may want to study a subject just for fun. It really is a personal decision, and I only hope that you gain as much from your study as I did mine.

In summary, when researching the course or qualification you're interested in, consider the following:

- How much does it cost?
- Is a deposit required?
- Are there set dates?
- Are there any prerequisites?
- What qualification or certificate will you achieve at the end?
- Is it part-time or full-time?
- Where would you undertake the course?
- Is the course "self-paced"?
- What is required in the form of coursework and assessment?
- What is the duration of the course?
- Is there any team or group work involved?
- Can this offer me a new career?

List below the preferred course or professional qualifications you're interested in undertaking.

_____

_____

_____

What would you like to achieve from gaining a professional qualification?

_____

_____

_____

How would having this qualification make a difference in your life or work?

_____

_____

_____

Where Do You Want to Go?

Next, you need to consider where you would like to spend your career break, but first let's do a quick recap. So far, you have identified your big *why*, reviewed your values and how you are going to make decisions to support them, discovered your preferred travel style, and identified some of the experiences you would like to have. So now it's time to think about *where* you want to go and what you want to do in the countries you'd like to visit.

If you've been thinking about travelling for a while, then you may have already read travel guides, researched on the internet, bought maps, and talked to lots of people. You may also have a firm idea of where you want to go and what you want to do, although your thoughts may have changed after completing the exercises throughout this book.

With so many options available, it's tough deciding where to go. You might want to see as many countries as possible or focus on one particular region. So, what is *your* travel strategy?

The purpose of this exercise it to help you to identify your travel strategy and what experiences – given the exercises you completed earlier where you identified your travel style and preferred type of travel – you would like to have in the countries of your choice. For example:

Where do you want to go?	What experience(s) would you like to have there?
Thailand	• Hill tribe trekking • Try your hand at cooking the local cuisine • Take a tut-tuk around Bangkok • Try the local rum, Sang-Sum • Volunteer in an elephant sanctuary in Chiang Mai • Attempt to learn some of the local language
Dominican Republic	• Volunteer work in an orphanage • Lie on the beach • Taste the local cuisine • Interact with the locals • Visit the Museo Alcázar de Colón
Australia	• Meet some "fair-dinkum" Aussies • Visit Uluru • Volunteer on a marine conservation on the Great Barrier Reef • Cuddle a koala • Learn a few Aussie phrases • Dive the Great Barrier Reef
Caribbean	• Lie on a beach and relax • Work on your tan • Drink cocktails
Egypt	• Visit the pyramids • Take a cruise down the Nile • Enter the tomb of King Tutankhamun • Buy some of the locally made rugs
Italy	• Learn Italian • Visit historical monuments • Take an Italian cooking class • Taste the local vino
Kenya	• Teach English at a local school • Learn how to make local food • Go on a safari • Learn some of the local language

Galapagos Islands	• Have a photo taken with the largest tortoises in the world • Swim with baby sea lions • Volunteer on a marine conservation project • Take a cruise around the islands, visiting the local habitat and bird life
San Francisco	• Drive over the Golden Gate Bridge • Take a train ride to Napa Valley • Head down to Pier 39 for some crab • Ride the scenic cable car across town • Spend hours in Yosemite National Park

Now it's your turn. Taking into consideration your travel style and the travel experiences you would like to have, in the table below write down *where you want to go* and *what experiences you would like to have*.

Where do you want to go?	**What experiences would you like to have there?**

How do you feel about what you identified on your list above?

_____

_____

_____

Are there any further actions you need to take to help you decide where to go and what experiences you would like to have?

_____

_____

_____

Who will support you to achieve what you have identified?

_____

_____

_____

Resources

If you're looking for further resources, Meet, Plan, Go! offer a basic training curriculum for only $149 (USD), where you receive eight self-paced lessons, ongoing community forum and access, and the opportunity to connect with like-minded peers. Here's an outline of the course contents.

1. Finding Your Inspiration
2. From Inspiration to Reality... Next steps
3. Earn your Freedom. Financial Planning for Long-Term World Travel
4. Alternatives to Traditional Tourism
5. Own Your Journey
6. Essential "To Do" Lists, Items for the Road

7. "To Do's" for Home and Career

8. Two for the Road. Tying It Together and Next Steps

Read the testimonials from those who have joined the programme, find out your role in the programme, and meet the instructors. Visit Meet, Plan, Go! at www.meetplango.com/basic-training/curriculum.

Summary

I hope you now have a very clear idea of your travel style, discovered the types of experiences available to you, and gained some insight into where you want to go and the experience(s) you want to have. All of these elements will have a direct impact on the outcome of your travels and, of course, how much you will enjoy your experiences. It may be that you can't go everywhere you want to in the time frame of your career break, but no need to worry: you can save the remainder for your second or maybe third break! Right now, prioritise what's really important to you, and focus on what's realistically achievable. Remember to consider your budget, your travel style, and what you're prepared to compromise on if your initial desires are unavailable. It's always a good idea to have a backup plan to avoid disappointment.

If you've read "My Story" at the back of the book, you'll notice I allowed myself the opportunity to be flexible and take advantage of any offers that presented themselves. If I had my entire career breaks planned out, I may have missed some amazing experiences. For example, during my first career break I hadn't planned to go to Taiwan. However, when I was in Australia I tracked down an old school friend, Samantha, and found she was living in Taiwan with her husband but was in northern Thailand completing a Thai massage course. Luckily, I was flying to Bangkok the following week and we managed to meet up. Samantha then invited me to Taiwan (how could I say no?), and after a quick phone call to my airline, I changed my flight back to the UK and ended up staying in Taiwan for a month sight-seeing, spending time with my friends, and volunteering at a children's home.

Where you go, what you do and for how long is your choice. You may prefer to plan your entire trip in advance or prefer to see what opportunities present themselves. This may depend on how long you have and what you want to achieve in that time. Best to be realistic about what approach best suits you.

Chapter 6:

IF YOU WANT TO STAY AT HOME

Staying at home for your career break is certainly an option. There are no set rules or guidelines that stipulate that you have to go abroad. In fact, one of the most common reasons that women take a career break is to have a baby. However, if you are not going to be busy looking after a baby during your career break, there are lots of options available to you.

Options

- Relax
- Volunteering
- Evaluating a career change
- Learning a new skill or language
- Studying or gaining a professional qualification
- Renovating your property
- Writing a book
- Undertaking part-time work or work experience

Let's consider these options in more detail.

Relax

Finally you can chill out and relax! When was the last time you sat around in your PJs all day? Or spent hours in the park, sitting under your favourite tree, reading your favourite book? Or had time to clear out the garage or paint that spare room? Doing nothing during your career break is a great way to recharge your batteries, have time to yourself, and sort out those niggling things that you never seem to have time for. Your time will really be *yours,* and how you spend it will be totally up to you. You may be like Bal Madhar, who chose to spend the remaining time of her career break planning her wedding. Of course, that requires a fiancé and a wedding to plan!

Alison Light spent her entire eight-month career break at home after resigning from a job that had left her with very little personal time. Alison revelled in not having to get up in the morning and go to work, much to the resentment of her husband. Alison says cheekily, "I did get out of bed in the morning; it just happened to be after my husband left for work, so he never saw it."

During her time off, Alison dedicated herself to making the perfect scone. She regrets how many mistakes she made, as she was then forced to eat them all. Yes, Alison, we feel your pain! She then went on to learn how to make lemon curd, decorate her house, spend quality time with her family (which she hadn't had time for since she left school), be on call to babysit her godson during the week, drink copious amounts of coffee, and boast how her house had never been so clean, which her husband didn't resent her for at all. During this time, Alison says, she felt "things were the way things should be" and even admitted she loved being a housewife and, whilst saying this, humbly apologised for not being a feminist.

Alison also took refuge in her garden and found herself starting to dig it up. She soon realized she loved being outside seeing things grow and being more creative. This led her to acknowledge that she didn't want to go back to working in human resources, and especially not into banking. Alison found she had an interest in garden design and realised she could use the project planning skills she'd accumulated, but with a creative twist. She began her search for a garden design course; however, on looking into this in more detail, saw that the cost of retraining full-time was more than expected, so she had to return to work.

The difference this time is that she went back to work part-time, and not in banking, which allowed her one day a week to focus on her study. She found a job that allowed her the work–life balance that was lacking in her previous role and was delighted that she was arriving home before dark. Alison's goal is to earn enough money to complete a full-time course in garden design.

I asked Alison what the best thing was about her career break. She said finding something that she was genuinely inspired by and finding the work–life balance in her new job she never thought was achievable in London." Interestingly, Alison's plan to "do nothing" led to a change of career and an improvement in work–life balance.

Tracey Baldwyn took her first career break at the age of forty-four, though had been thinking about it since she was forty. As mentioned earlier, Tracey worked as procurement manager in London, in a demanding, pressurised, and stressful environment. Tracey was at the top of her field, enjoying seniority, the compensation package that came with her job, and credibility and respect in the industry. But this all came at a price, and when making her final decision to make the break, Tracey took these points into consideration:

- She felt she was never able to switch off.
- She felt constantly stressed and worn out.
- She didn't get the same "buzz" from work that it used to provide.
- She was fed up working long hours, both in the office and at home.
- She found herself eating convenience-based food as she had no time to cook.
- She felt fatigued and tired.
- She spent the weekend doing chores, which left little time for entertaining or seeing friends and family.

- She didn't have much quality time to spend with her husband.

In the end, Tracey extended her career break from six to nine months and really benefitted from taking time for herself, both physically and mentally. She did have initial feelings of guilt and insecurity about the future, which were not helped by the attitude of others. Tracey believes it would have been more acceptable to others if she had taken time off to travel or undertake volunteer work, rather than "do nothing." It has now been almost ten years since Tracey took her first career break, and since then she has taken a few more, which you'll find more about in the section "Renovating a Property." In hindsight, Tracey wishes she'd had the courage to take her first career break earlier than she did; she understands the fear that people go through when agonising over the decision to make the break.

If, like Tracey, you're feeling fear over taking a career break, then refer back to "Chapter 4: Making It Happen," where we addressed that issue.

Volunteering

Volunteering is not just an option for those going abroad. There are many organisations right on your doorstep who would be more than willing to accept your help. You could get involved in mentoring teenagers, chopping up vegetables in an old people's home, reading books to primary school children, or working in a charity shop. On his return from climbing Mt Kilimanjaro, Ted Harrington found himself volunteering at a local charity and found the experience highly rewarding.

Like Ted, you may have already found a volunteer organisation or project to work on. However, if you're still reviewing your options, then here are some suggestions.

Volunteer with young people

- **Chance UK** – www.chanceuk.com
- **Get connected** – www.getconnected.org.uk
- **Save the Children** – www.savethechildren.org.uk

Volunteer with animals:

- **Volunteer London** –www.static.london.gov.uk/volunteer/ things/animals.jsp
- **Animal Care & Control of NYC** - www.nycacc.org
- **RSPCA** –www.rspca.org.uk/getinvolved/volunteer
- **International Animal Rescue** – www.internationalanimalrescue.org

Volunteer with the aged

- **Elder Helpers** - www.elderhelpers.org
- **Age UK** –www.ageuk.org.uk
- **Contact the Elderly** –www.contact-the-elderly.org.uk
- **Healthy Years** –www.healthyyears.org

Evaluating a Career Change

Time out of your career gives you time to re-evaluate your values, goals, and career path and to ascertain your career is really giving you what you want. It also gives you the opportunity to explore alternative career options and make the changes you desire. If this sounds like you, then you may be wondering where to start your search. Changing careers can be a big step, and you want to ensure you have all the tools to be in a position to make an informed decision.

Although Tracey Baldywn was officially "doing nothing" on her career break, she did spend time re-evaluating her career. She pondered making some changes, such as a move into floristry or property development, but realised she actually liked what she did, though this time round would return as a contractor as opposed to taking on permanent roles. Appreciating that contracting would not provide the same sort of job and financial security she had enjoyed in the past, Tracey felt this time round she just wanted to get on with her job, sidestep all the office politics and corporate responsibilities, and enter her new job in the mind-set that she would only be in roles for a specific amount of time which made her feel more in control and independent. Tracey never returned to permanent work and has continued to contract, enjoying the psychological freedom that comes with this type of work, and she now approaches her work with renewed enthusiasm and eagerness.

Tracey came to her conclusion by herself; however, it may be that you need someone to talk to and help you get very clear on your thoughts and next steps. One course of action is securing the services of a career coach. A career coach will help you identify your career goals and aspirations and discuss some of your preferred options. Exercises and tools you might use include psychometric tests, the wheel of life, value elicitation, goal setting, reviewing and refreshing your CV, addressing issues around self-confidence and limiting beliefs, and identifying obstacles that could hold you back.

There are some specialist career break coaches, myself included, coaching people just like you who have taken, or are planning to take, a career break and are now looking for their next move. My expertise lies in having worked in recruitment for over twelve years and having taken two career breaks in the last six years, so I am well placed to understand your thoughts, feelings and mind-set, before, during and after your career break. Here are some other options, depending on your location.

USA

- **Institute for Coaching** – www.instituteforcoaching.com
- **Career Intervention** – www.careerintervention.com

- **Career Coach USA** – www.careercoachusa.net

Australia

- **Total Balance** – www.totalbalance.com.au
- **Amazing Results** – www.amazingresults.com.au
- **Carnegie Management Group** – www.carnegiemg.com.au

Canada

- **Career Joy** – www.careerjoy.com
- **Canada Career Coach** – www.canadacareercoach.com
- **Feroce Coaching** – www.ferocecoaching.com

United Kingdom

- **Find a Life Coach** – www.findalifecoach.co.uk
- **The Career Coach** – www.thecareercoach.co.uk
- **Amazing People** – www.amazingpeople.co.uk

If you're based in the UK, another option for you is Careershifters. org, the UK's leading dedicated online career change guide. They have compiled practical advice from some of the country's top career change experts to help you make a successful shift. Whether you're just thinking about a change or you've already started the process, these nuggets of expert wisdom will help you create a career that really gets you going. If you subscribe to their newsletter, you're immediately sent a "25 Top Tips to Kick-Start Your Career Change" document for free.

They also offer a workshop designed to help you through those first essential stages of changing career: figuring out what you really want and making a realistic action plan. Visit their website for more details www.careershifters.org.

And if that isn't enough, you can also purchase their e-book, in which you will learn

- the seven key steps to making a successful career change;
- how to discover the work that will make you truly happy;
- the secrets to turning your dream career into a living;
- the five things that stop most people making a successful career change;
- how to be sure that you've made the right career choice;
- how to make a career change plan and stick to it;
- how to handle your finances when changing career; and
- what to do when you get stuck.

Learning a New Skill or a New Language

Local colleges, community centres, and independent schools offer so many courses you'll be pressed to choose among salsa lessons, a creative writing class, learning how to take the ultimate photo, or speaking Italian, French, or Spanish. You could always combine a few and really add some additional skills to your life's tool kit, whilst having a bit of fun. If you don't know where to begin, then here are some websites to get you started, no matter where you live.

Photography Courses

- **Photography Institute** – www.thephotographyinstitute.co.uk
- **Photoprenuer** – www.blogs.photopreneur.com/top-photography-schools-in-the-usa-to-learn-photography
- **School of Photography** – www.schoolofphotography.com
- **New York Institute of Photography** – www.nyip.com
- **Photography Courses** – www.photography-courses.com.au

Cooking Courses

- **Cooking School Guide** – www.cookingschoolguide.com
- **Ashburton Cookery School** – www.ashburtoncookeryschool.co.uk
- **Cooking Schools of America** – www.cookingschoolsofamerica.com
- **Cooking School Guide** – cookingschoolguide.com
- **Thai Cooking School** – www.thaicookeryschool.com

Language Courses

- **Cactus Language** – www.cactuslanguage.com/en
- **Language Schools Worldwide** – www.lsw-languages.com
- **UIC London** – www.uiclondon.com
- **Language Study Go Abroad** – www.languagestudy.goabroad.com
- **Studying in Australia** – www.studyingaustralia.com

Studying for a Professional Qualification

You may have wanted to complete some study for a long time, however, other "life things" got in your way, and now you've decided it's time to get that qualification under your belt. If you are planning to complete a degree, then become familiar with the university system, what's required to make an application, and when to submit your application. Speak to their careers service, or even make an appointment to speak to someone face to face. If you've planned your career break around your study, you certainly want to ensure all the relevant paperwork and supporting documents are sufficient. Consider how you'd feel if your application wasn't accepted purely due to an oversight on the application form!

The same principles apply for any course you're thinking about undertaking. Plan your career break around the start and end dates, and ensure you leave enough time to complete any assignments or coursework. Completing a PhD was something Erika Langham (from Bagara, Queensland, Australia) had aspired to for a long time (since her early twenties). She thought seriously about it for a few years, but working as a senior consultant, with two small children and a husband who was deployed half of the year, she knew it wasn't the right time. When the global financial crisis hit, she had ventured out as an independent consultant, and in the space of about two weeks, she saw all the work she had lined up for the next year fall through. Suddenly it seemed as if the time was right. For Erika and her family, losing a consultant's salary to a scholarship involved a lot of economising; however, they believe they've gained a lot by the reduced income, with increased family time and less wastage. They have vowed to make better use of their money when Erika is earning again. Erika hopes that she has chosen her PhD topic well enough that she will be employable at the end; she has worked with people whose PhD topics are highly specialised or not relevant to their career, and as such struggle to find work in their desired field. The goal in doing a PhD was never about monetary gain or career enhancement – she thinks both of those have actually gone backwards – it was always a personal goal, allowing her to sink into the sheer joy of learning, and a side effect was gaining the flexibility to better meet the needs of her children.

After living in Australia for some time, Vicky Gardner decided she wanted a change of career from the hospitality industry. Whilst Vicky was in her teens, her mum qualified as an aromatherapist, and she'd been intrigued by the "natural health" fields since then. Aromatherapy was on the list of skills needed in Australia, so Vicky started her research into the subject and industry. It also meant that if she decided to move back to the UK, it was a qualification she could take with her and would be recognized.

Once Vicky had made her decision, she did lots of research into which schools and courses were recognised by Australia's immigration department, as she also wanted to ensure she had a backup plan if her application for permanent residency failed.

To become qualified, Vicky completed six different courses. She states she occasionally felt lost and that studying full-time wasn't for her. Financially, things became tough with no income, and without permanent residency, handouts from the government were nonexistent. Then the fear of standing on her own two feet started to emerge, and with no family to support the thought of launching her own business became a little unsettling as she came closer to qualifying in all her courses.

Vicky didn't let her fear get the better of her, and after completing her studies and qualifying as an aromatherapist, she made the transition to the natural health and massage field and started her own business. She says she finally felt in control of her life and her destiny!

Running her own business hasn't always been easy, as whilst working *in* the business you cannot work *on* the business, and this is a struggle for many small business owners. However, the journey has definitely been worthwhile! It has opened many other doors that would have remained closed, and some amazing other opportunities have presented themselves along the way.

Taking a career break to further your education can be an impressive contribution to your CV. It may be viewed favourably by your current employer or even your new one, especially if it helps you in your role. If you're like Vicky and you undertake study to change your career, it can allow you the freedom to start a whole new chapter in your career and maybe even become your own boss.

You may already have been thinking about what, and where, you want to study, though if you're in the early stages and still considering your options, then the sites below may be helpful.

United Kingdom

- **The Open University** – www.open.ac.uk
- **Study London** – www.studylondon.ac.uk
- **London Development Agency** – www.lda.gov.uk/our-work/promoting-London/studying-in-London/index.aspx

USA

- **Universities in the USA** – www.universitiesintheusa.com
- **America Study Guide** – www.americastudyguide.com
- **Study in America** – www.studyinamerica.com

Australia

- **Study in Australia** – www.studyinaustralia.gov.au/Sia/en/Home.htm
- **Australian Universities** – www.australian-universities.com
- **Grad School** – www.gradschool.com.au

Renovating Your Property

DIY on weekends seems to take forever, right? If you're looking to speed up the renovation work on your property, or even an investment property, then taking some time out might be the best option to get the job done quickly and efficiently. Plus, if you've hired workmen, you can keep an eye on them to ensure they get the work done. If you've never renovated a property, then it would be advisable to do as much research as possible before embarking on such a big, potentially very expensive and time-consuming, task. Designs on Property (www.designsonproperty.co.uk/categories/renovate-a-home-top-ten-dos-and-donts) suggest that you carefully plan and budget for your renovation and offer some suggestions on how best to manage your project.

Whether you're looking for inspiration, ideas, or recommendations, there is certainly no shortage of shows, websites, and courses to get those creative juices flowing to build the home of your dreams or start your property empire. So, whatever stage you're at, here are some sites to get you started or provide you with more information:

- **Property Renovate** – www.propertyrenovate.com
- **Renovation Riches** – www.renovationriches.com

- **Homebuilding and Renovating** – www.homebuilding.co.uk
- **Home Concepts** – www.homeconcepts.co.uk
- **Buy Associate** – www.buyassociation.co.uk
- **Your Property Club** – www.property-course.yourpropertyclub.com/2/

Tracey Baldwyn renovated her first property during her second career break, at the age of forty-six. Tracey had always been interested in property renovation and, as she was now contracting, as opposed to working in a permanent role, found she could take some time off between contracts to gain the experience of renovating a property, with the intention and hope of making a profit.

Tracey and her husband purchased a property, and over the course of a few months they renovated it, sold it, and made some money in the meantime. Tracey says she loved it and whilst she acknowledges that a contract in procurement would have been far more profitable, she doesn't regret if for a second. She learned some new skills, and although there was an initial element of fear and she made some mistakes, she found it both challenging and exciting. Tracey and her husband have since gone on to renovate and sell more properties.

Writing a Book

Is there a crime writer in you dying to get out? Are you a Mills and Boon fan and long to write a love story of your own? Or maybe you've been inspired by *Master Chef* and have a few secret recipes of your own you'd like to share with the world. You may already have the skills of a professional writer and know all the "ins and outs" of the publishing world. However, if you're a novice, then there are many courses available to you which will help you prepare for the creation and development, marketing, and publication sides of your venture. Who knows, your book may even become a best seller!

188 | Sue Hadden

You have probably gathered by now that I started writing this book during my second career break. I started writing it while I was back in Australia and finished it in the UK, at the tail end of my career break ... and beyond!

I'm sure it's also not going to be a shock that the concept of my book came about through my love of coaching and career breaks. When I'm asked how it came about, it's hard to recall the exact moment when the idea popped into my head. All I know is that once the idea was there, I couldn't get it out of my head and felt compelled to do something about it. Maybe you feel the same way about a subject? The more I wrote, the more I loved what I was doing; the more people I talked to, the more time I spent researching; the more I asked people to read my drafts, the more contributions I asked for; and the list goes on. The end result of being published was always present; however, the drive for me was more around my passion and desire to help and encourage other people to make the break and experience all the wonderful things taking a career break brings.

From personal experience I believe writing a book requires the following.

- *Ideas* – you may have a few ideas churning around in your head that could possibly be turned into a book. Study the market and see if anyone has published anything similar. If the market is saturated with books on the subject, then maybe choose another one of your ideas.

- *Find a niche* – write something unique that has never been done before.

- *Passion* – is there something you are passionate about? Do you have a story to tell or an opinion to share? If you don't have passion, you won't finish your book.

- *Inspiration* – either from yourself or others. Without inspiration, your book will only ever stay an idea or a draft.

- *Commitment* – you need to be fully committed to the idea of completing the book if you want to get published. Many people start writing a book, but not many people finish, so have an end result in mind, and once you've made the decision, commit to it. There have been quite a few times during my journey when I've just wanted to be a couch potato, turn on the TV, and do nothing, but a little internal voice would give me a kick-start.

- *Time* – do not underestimate the amount of time required to write a book. Depending on your topic, you may need to undertake research, ask for contributions, conduct interviews, source an editor and publisher, and so much more. During my career break, I had the freedom to write every day. When I returned to London and ventured back into full-time work, my time was somewhat limited. Whilst my goal was to finish the book as soon as possible, I also wanted to ensure I achieved some sort of balance, so I committed to writing one day per weekend, and on occasion both days, though this did depend on social arrangements. I did not want to compromise on the integrity of the book and the material, so if the book took longer to write than anticipated, I was prepared to accept that.

- *Resources* – having a PC or laptop aids in getting your ideas down, plus you can save your work.

- *Friends* – people to bounce your ideas off or ask to read your drafts

- *Money* – depending on how you wish your book to be published, it may be you need to pay for it to be published.

If the concept of writing a book seems a bit daunting, then book yourself into a writing course. A course may provide you with some guidance and structure on how to start your journey. Depending on where you live, here are some suggestions.

Courses in the UK

- **Writers Bureau** – www.writersbureau.com
- **London School of Journalism** – www.lsj.org
- **Complete Creative Writing Course** – www.writingcourses. org.uk

Courses in the USA

- **Writing Classes** – www.writingclasses.com
- **Freelance Writing** – www.freelance-writing.net/romance-writing.htm
- **Media Bistro** – www.mediabistro.com/courses/cache/crs6083.asp

Courses in Australia

- **Sydney Writers Centre** – www.sydneywriterscentre.com.au/creativewriting.htm
- **Study Now** – www.studynow.com.au/Creative-Writing-Course.html
- **Hot Courses** – www.hotcourses.com.au/australia/home.html

Other Worldwide Locations

- **Dark Angels, Spain** – www.dark-angels.org.uk/advanced.htm
- **Grub Street, Boston** – www.grubstreet.org/
- **Canadian Universities, Canada** – www.canadian-universities.net/Universities/Programs/Creative_Writing.html
- **Collaldra School of Writing, Italy** – www.collaldraschoolofwriting.com/blog
- **Creative Writing, Chicago** – creativewriting.uchicago.edu
- **Write Away Travel** – www.writeawaytravel.com

If you think there's a book in you, then I would definitely encourage you to get out your PC or a pad and pen and start writing. What with all the resources available to you, there's no time like the present to get started. You don't know what you're capable of if you don't try, right?

Part-time Work or Work Experience

Taking on part-time work will depend on the arrangements made with your employer. If you resigned from your job to take a career break, then you are free to take on part-time work, or any work, for that matter. However, if you've taken a sabbatical, then you may not be able to participate in any other form of paid work. You should check with your manager or study your sabbatical policy before making any form of commitment.

You could get around this by doing some unpaid work. This is a great opportunity for you to experience a new line of work or a new industry, which may encourage you to enter a new career.

If you need help, take a look at these sites:

- **A Career Change** –www.acareerchange.co.uk/finding-work-experience-adult.html

- **No Limits** – www.no-limits.org.uk/latest-news/story/clitheroe-business-finds-work-experience-for-adults

- **Manchester City Council** – www.manchester.gov.uk/info/500190/careers_in_social_care/4508/support_for_adults-work_experience_placements/1

- **Australia's Careers On-line** – www.careersonline.com.au/show/next.html

In summary, staying at home during a career break can be either highly productive or very relaxing, or maybe you can squeeze in a combination of both. As with Ted, Tracey, and Erika, whatever you choose to do must be right for you.

Chapter 7:

TAKING CARE OF YOURSELF

Managing Stress

Everyone, at some point in their lives, experiences stress. Whilst stress can be positive and energise us to achieve goals and stay focused, it also has another side that can make our lives difficult, to say the least. Even though taking a career break is an exciting adventure, planning and executing the break may at some point cause you some stress. Whether the stress be financial, family, friends, or career, it's important to be able to recognise the signs and manage them immediately.

Watch out for:

- Headaches and migraines
- Sleeping difficulties
- Feelings of anxiety and worry
- Lack of appetite or comfort eating
- Not enjoying things you normally would
- Irritability and snappiness
- Being clumsy and more forgetful than usual
- Recurrent sickness such as colds, flu, chest infections
- Aches and pains
- Excessive drinking or smoking
- Becoming a recluse and not seeing your friends

Strategies for overcoming stress:

- Increasing exercise—walking, gym, swimming
- Practising yoga or Pilates
- Eating a healthy, balanced diet
- Limiting alcohol and smoking
- Getting away for a weekend—fresh air and country walks
- Getting more sleep
- Talking over your problems with a friend or a professional

For me, I talk things over with friends, family members, or fellow coaches. I also like to write things down in a journal so I can see my fears, issues and concerns in black and white and on paper. Another strategy that works for me is exercise. OK, I may be stretching the truth here unless you count walking to a coffee shop exercise.

List some of the strategies you can utilize if you start feeling stressed.

1. _____
2. _____
3. _____
4. _____
5. _____

It may be that one of your strategies is securing the services of a coach to help you through these stressful times. As already noted in chapter 6, "Staying at Home," here are some coaching organisations.

United Kingdom

- **Find a Life Coach** – www.findalifecoach.co.uk
- **The Career Coach** – www.thecareercoach.co.uk
- **Amazing People** – www.amazingpeople.co.uk

USA

- **Institute for Coaching** – www.instituteforcoaching.com
- **Career Intervention** – www.careerintervention.com
- **Career Coach USA** – www.careercoachusa.net

Australia

- **Total Balance** – www.totalbalance.com.au
- **Amazing Results** – www.amazingresults.com.au
- **Carnegie Management Group** – www.carnegiemg.com.au

Celebrate Your Success

It's important to celebrate your success when you achieve one of your goals. Maybe just buy yourself your favourite chocolate or a magazine, but acknowledge how hard you've worked to achieve your goal, and then reward yourself. This will help to keep you motivated to continue to achieve your other goals.

If you have a best friend, or a group of close friends, call them, go out for a drink, and share with them your decision and exciting new plans. Remember to surround yourself with people who are going to support your decision, keep you motivated, and be there for you when times get tough.

How will you celebrate your success?

_____

_____

_____

_____

_____

_____

Chapter 8:

PULLING IT ALL TOGETHER

Reviewing Your Successes

Our journey together is coming to an end, and as we get out the box of tissues, let's reflect on some of the ideas, thoughts, and decisions you've made, and recognise just how far you've come.

Your big **why.** You've identified your reasons for wanting to take a career break, become very clear in your intentions, discovered what could hold you back, and recognized how you will overcome any obstacles.

Your new values. To achieve your career break, you reviewed and created a set of values that will support and sustain you to achieve your dream. You also identified how your new values will impact your lifestyle and the decisions you now make towards attaining your goal.

Mind over matter. By using simple techniques you are now able to reframe any negative thoughts that may hinder your moving forward in the attainment of your goal.

What can hold you back from taking a career break. By identifying your limiting beliefs you are now able to overcome them by restating them, using empowering statements and strategies to embed them into your subconscious, so that they become your new personal beliefs.

Creating your goals. Using the SMART model for goal setting, you created your new goals and the keys to achieving your outcome, which will bring the results you're looking for.

Be, Do, Have. You successfully identified who you need to be and what you need to do in order to have the experience you want to invite into your life.

Your Travel Style. With so many elements to consider when travelling during your career break, you successfully filtered a host of styles to determine your preferred style, identified what you can and can't live without, and are now more aware of all the styles available to you.

Types of experiences you want – you successfully determined what travel experiences you wish to have during your career break and with so many to choose from, you may have identified a few things you want to achieve or be involved in when you're there.

Where you want to go – with the world being your oyster, you've become clearer in deciding where you want to go during your career break.

What you want to do – after deciding where you want to go, you identified what you'd like to do and which activities you'd like to experience. You may find once you're there, other exciting opportunities come your way.

If you stay at home, what you will do – you identified what you want to achieve if you're staying at home during your career break. You may now even be thinking about combining a few activities to really make the most of your break.

Managing stress– you've recognized that you may experience stress or other health concerns during the planning and execution of your career break, and have identified strategies to overcome these.

Celebrating your success – by celebrating your success, you're acknowledging a milestone in the attainment of your goals. Plus, you've identified just how you're going to celebrate and with whom you're going to share your success. So, start planning your party ☺

There is one last action you need to take.

Make a commitment!

I, _____

(your name), hereby commit to turning my dreams and desires into reality by undertaking the necessary steps towards taking a career break.

Date: _____

Your Signature: _____

Witness 1 (friend, relative, co-worker who will support you in your dreams)

Date: _____

Signature: _____

Witness 2 (friend, relative, co-worker who will support you in your dreams)

Date: _____

Signature: _____

Before we end our time together, let's revisit why you chose this book and see whether it provided you with what you were looking for. Your Career Break: the *'how to'* guide aimed to:

1. help you identify whether a career break really is for you and why

2. provide you with strategies to overcome the psychological barriers that may hold you back

3. help you get specific about where you want to go and what you want to do

This how-to guide provided you with:

1. exercises to help keep you focused, motivated, and committed to achieving your goals

2. quotes, statistics, and information to assist you in making informed decisions along your journey

3. real-life examples from myself and others who have "made the break" and lived to tell the tale (emotionally, physically, and financially!)

On reviewing your answers to the questions and exercises throughout the book, ask yourself these questions:

- Did I discover the reason(s) I wanted to take a career break?

- Did I identify whether a career break really is for me and why?

- Am I clear in my decision to either ask for a sabbatical or resign from my job?

- Is my *why* powerful enough?

- Have I created strategies to overcome any psychological issues that may arise?

- Are my values now aligned to my goals?

- Have I identified strategies to maintain momentum in order to achieve my goals?

- Have I decided how long my career break will be?
- Am I clear about where I want to go and what I want to do?
- Do I know how much money I need?
- Have I identified those who will support me in my journey?

I hope the answer to all these questions is *yes* and that you are now very clear about what you want to do and that you know how to achieve it.

Thank you for taking me on this journey with you and allowing me to be a part of your dreams. I hope by completing the exercises in the book and reading the stories from contributors it has cemented your desire to make the break. Go on, make the commitment and live your dreams!

Good luck in your onwards journey and adventures.

Sue

REFERENCES

Joe Bindloss, "Volunteering", Wanderlust: Guide to Career Breaks, (2010), 13-17

Joe Bindloss, "Working", Wanderlust: Guide to Career Breaks, (2010), 10-12

Charlotte Hindle, "It is time for a break?", Wanderlust: Guide to Career Breaks, (2010), 2-3

Griffiths, S. (2008). *Gap Year for Grown Ups (3rd edition)*. Crimson Publishing.

Youell, R. & Youell, C. (2011). *Effective NLP skills*. Kogan Page Limited.

Websites and Internet sources

www.abc7.com

www.alexisgrant.com

www.answers.com

www.aviva-sa.com

www.ayutthaya-boat.com

www.blueventures.org

www.briefcasetobackpack.com

www.bsigroup.com

www.businessdictionary.com

www.canada.com

www.careerbreakcafe.com

www.careerbreaksecrets.com

www.careershifters.org

www.deccanchronicle.com

www.designsonproperty.co.uk

www.elance.com

www.everyinvestor.co.uk

www.ezinearticles.com

www.fierceinc.com

www.freepursuits.com (www.corbettbarr.com)

www.french.china.org.cn

www.gapadvice.org

www.gapyearforgrownups.co.uk

www.geckosadventures.com

www.haveinternetwilltravel.com

www.homeschoolblogger.com

www.i-to-i.com

www.intrepidtravel.com

www.madagascar.co.uk

www.madventurer.com

www.mindtools.com

www.meetplango.com

www.mondochallenge.co.uk

www.money.usnews.com

www.news.efinancialcareers.co.uk

www.nutty-adventures.com

www.odesk.com

www.originalvolunteers.co.uk

www.peopleperhour.com

www.projects-abroad.co.uk

www.raleighinternational.org

www.responsibletourismawards.com
(www.responsibletravel.com/awards)

www.responsibletravel.com

www.sanccob.co.za

www.statistics.gov.uk

www.thecareerbreaksite.com

www.the-coaching-academy.com

www.theexpeditioner.com

www.thefreedictionary.com

www.threemonthvisa.com

www.traveltrends.biz

www.useconomy.about.com

www.voluntaryworker.co.uk

www.whatsonwhen.com

www.wikipedia.com

www.workingabroadmagazine.com

www.volunteerlatinamerica.com

www.worklifebliss.com.au

www.yearoutgroup.org

www.yomps.co.uk

www.yoursabbatical.com

www.zenhabits.net

APPENDICES

MY STORY

A friend suggested I include this section; he thought it would be beneficial for you to know what has led me to where I am today and to share my career break and travel stories. It would be easy for me to ramble for pages, so to avoid this, I have structured this section into a Q&A format.

Why Have I Taken Career Breaks?

I had never really considered taking a career break until I had my first one back in October 2005. It wasn't a conscious decision. I left one of my jobs in banking that came with a nice lump sum of cash. The way I saw it, I had two choices: 1) find another job or 2) take a break and go travelling. For me, it was a no-brainer!

My second career break was planned almost two years before I actually left the UK. My intention was to take at least one year off, so I knew I needed quite of lot of money to sustain my break. The reason for this break was to return to Australia to spend quality time with my family, as my sister has four kids and I'd been away, living in London for ten years. I felt it really was time to head home and see my family.

Where Have I Been on My Career Breaks, and What Have I Done ?

As mentioned, I have taken two career breaks in the last six years. Here's the breakdown:

Break One: _six months (October 2005–March 2006), age thirty-five_

- Three months in Los Angeles upskilling my photography, going on photo shoots, spending time in San Francisco, Las Vegas, Sedona, and the Grand Canyon
- Six weeks in Australia visiting family and friends, spending time in Airlie Beach, Sydney, Brisbane, and the Sunshine Coast
- One month in Thailand, travelling north and then down south to the islands
- One month in Taiwan volunteering at a children's home just outside Ei-lan; three days in Hong Kong on the way back to the UK

Break Two: eighteen months (February 2009–August 2010), age thirty-eight

- Thirteen months living in Brisbane (Australia), which included seven months living with my sister and her four kids (what an experience!), three months living at the Gold Coast, then three months living back in Brisbane with friends; completed a Life Coaching Qualification with The Coaching Institute (TCI) in Melbourne, Australia; designed coaching workshops; and started writing this book
- Attended three other self-development and coaching training courses:
- Rachel Anastasi (a coach to coaches) "Unleash Your Secret Power" retreat in Philip Island, Victoria
- Chris Howard Training Academy Courses – Breakthrough to Success (Brisbane) and Rich Heart Wealthy Mind (Sydney)
- Attended a seminar by Brett McFall, author of _How to Make Money While You Sleep_ and internet entrepreneur, in addition to Brad Sugar, international entrepreneur, seminar

- Three months travelling through Asia (Vietnam, Laos, Cambodia, and Thailand). Whilst in Thailand I helped a friend redesign his website and write his tour programmes for his travel business
- Two months back in the UK (looking for a job)

Was I Clear about What I Wanted to Achieve on My Career Breaks?

Break One

I did have some plans but was open to change. I had pre-booked all my flights, two tours in Thailand, and some accommodation.

My original plan was:

- Two months in LA
- Six weeks in Australia
- One month in Thailand
- Three days in Hong Kong on the way back to London

What I actually did/achieved:

- Three months in LA upskilling my photography and travelling
- Six weeks in Australia spending time with family and friends
- One month in Thailand, spending time in the north and south
- One month in Taiwan visiting friends and volunteering at a children's home
- Three days in Hong Kong on the way back to London

I stayed longer in Los Angeles, due to an opportunity to get photography work experience, and added Taiwan into my plan, as I had regained contact with an old friend while in Australia, and she was now based in Taiwan. This turned out to be a very rewarding addition, as I spent a month volunteering at a children's home, which was a memorable experience.

To answer the question, I was clear to a certain extent about what I wanted to do and achieve in my first career break; however, I stayed flexible so I could alter my plans if something I wanted to do presented itself. I didn't have a job to return to, so I was in a position to change my plans. However, due to the flight I had originally booked with Trailfinders before I left, every time I changed my flights it cost me £50, which in the big scheme of things isn't a lot of money, though it's something to be aware of when booking flights.

Break Two

Career break two was planned almost two years before I left. I used to refer to it as my UK Exit Strategy. I had been living and working in London for ten years and, to be honest, was fed up with the weather, commuting, and the lifestyle and really needed a break. As I had been away for such a long time, I decided to return to Australia to spend time with my family. However, I didn't want to put a time frame on my break; therefore, I needed to ensure I had the funds necessary to sustain me. The two main ways I achieved this were by saving as much as I could each month, and by moving in with a friend so that I could rent out my flat for a year before I moved away. I booked a one-way flight to Brisbane, and the only plans I had were a six-day stop-over in Singapore, a week on Brampton Island, and a three-week cruise. The rest was all unknown!

My original plan was:

- Spend time with my family (no time limit)
- One week on Brampton Island
- Three-week cruise from Perth via Tasmania and New Zealand

What I actually did/achieved:

- One week on Brampton Island for a friend's birthday
- Three-week cruise from Perth to Sydney via Tasmania and New Zealand
- Seven months living in Brisbane with my sister, her husband, and her kids
- Visited friends in Cairns and visited Cape Tribulation
- One month in Vietnam
- One month in Laos and Cambodia
- One month in Bangkok staying with Thai friends and helping them with their travel business
- Three months living at the Gold Coast when I returned from Asia
- Three months living with friends in Brisbane before I returned to London
- Completed a Life Coaching Qualification with The Coaching Institute (TCI) in Melbourne, Australia
- Attended three other self-development and coaching training courses in Brisbane, Sydney, and Philip Island
- Started writing this book and wrote coaching workshops

Overall, I achieved and experienced so much more than I had originally set out to achieve, what with studying, completing extra courses, being able to support family and friends, reconnecting with friends I hadn't seen in nearly ten years, and travelling back to Asia. Even though this break wiped me out financially, I would not change one thing. Like I've said before, you can always earn more money (note to Dad!). The memories from my break will remain with me forever!

What Would I Do Differently?

During my second career break, I tended to stress about money on a regular basis, which was quite odd, as I had a substantial amount of money in the bank to finance it. I think it's just in my nature to worry about these things, though it was unnecessary at the time. What I found interesting is that I worried more when I had more, and worried less when I had less.

What Have Been the Benefits of My Career Breaks?

Wow, where do I start?

- Met like-minded people, some of whom have become great friends
- Experienced new cultures, customs, and religions
- Visited monumental places that carved our history
- Gave back to society through volunteer work
- Had time to reflect on what I wanted in life
- Became more understanding and tolerant of other people
- Learned new skills that can be transferred back in the workplace
- Reconnected with friends and family and therefore created tighter bonds
- Felt refreshed and enthused when I returned to the UK
- Gained a professional qualification that contributed to being offered a role based in New York
- Made me much more appreciative of what I have
- Lost attachments to my personal possessions
- Changed my mind-set on what's really important in life

Losing attachments to my personal possessions was the biggest shock for me. I conformed to the notion of the stereotypical woman, with a large collection of clothes, shoes, and bags, amongst other things. When I returned from my second career break, I went through all my boxes and culled approximately 80 percent of my wardrobe. I felt I didn't want to be bogged down with having so many material possessions, especially when some of the people I met through my travels had so little. It made me realize that I didn't need that much *stuff* to live. I do, however, appreciate we live in the western world, and in order to survive in our society and culture you need more material possessions; I decided I just didn't need as many as I thought. My uncle is the chairman at an Age Concern in Orpington (South East London), so I donated bags and bags to a local charity within Age Concern. For a few weeks he was a very popular man, turning up with lots of lovely items for them to sell.

The main benefit of my career breaks were how they contributed to being offered an international assignment in New York where I headed up the learning and development function for the company I was working for at the time of publishing this book. Living and working in New York had always been a dream and through becoming a coach and attending all the other coaching related workshops, I truly believe they had a direct impact on how my career progressed since returning to the UK in 2010.

I mentioned earlier in the book that whilst it took me a few months to secure a role on my return, I ended up in a position that was perfect for me and subsequently led to being offered an international assignment in a role that was the next natural step in my career. In this role I have the opportunity to utilise all the skills, knowledge and experience gained whilst training to become a coach and an NLP Practitioner so the investment I made in my own career and education, during my second career break and once I returned, has without a doubt, paid off.

What Are My Aspirations Going Forward?

My main goal is to make a difference in people's lives and help them do something they have always dreamed of doing. More specifically, I want to help as many people as possible take a career break, help them in their career decisions on their return, and help them successfully re-enter the workforce.

PERSONAL ACKNOWLEDGMENTS

When thinking about the people I wanted to acknowledge in this section, I focussed specifically on those who made an impact or contribution to my coaching journey and the creation and development of this book. I take pleasure in thanking the friends and family below.

Julie Greenwood, my beloved sister, who lives in Australia. She is quite proud of the fact that it was her "insightful" suggestion that I become a life coach. Without her insight, this book, and the journey I experienced to become a coach, would never have eventuated. Sis, a big thank-you and I love you always.

Debbie Norman has been one of my best friends since I arrived in London back in 1999. Debbie and I soon realised our compatibility when travelling, as we shared a love of shopping, wine, coffee, good food, and people watching. I thank Debbie for being a part of my life and sharing so many wonderful memories and experiences. She is a great listener and always very supportive.

Jacquie Honeyball is a friend I cannot imagine my life without. She is my rock and an amazing friend. Everyone should have a Jacquie in their lives. She has a naughty side, which she reveals only to those who are worthy. I am so glad I am worthy. Hugs.

Christine Allen is one sassy lady whom I met through becoming a life coach whilst in Australia. You know when you meet someone who is totally on your wavelength? Well, that's what happened with Chris. She listens and supports me but kicks my butt when required, and I promise you it's been required on quite a few occasions!

BIOGRAPHIES OF CONTRIBUTORS

My personal gratitude is extended to friends, family, acquaintances, and strangers (some who have been accosted in coffee shops, on planes and trains, in pubs, and on Facebook) who contributed, in one way or another, to this book. As this book took shape, I asked contributors for their "real-life" stories, anecdotes, words of wisdom, and general comments, feedback, and thoughts on their career break adventures. Each story is unique, just like the individual who experienced it. The purpose of asking for contributions was to share with you their trials, tribulations, and lessons learned – both good and bad. You will find that some career breakers have contributed to just one chapter, where others have shared their stories over a few chapters. Please let me introduce you to those who have provided their stories to help you:

Jon Stewart left the UK for greener pastures in 2008 and now lives in Hong Kong, working in recruitment advertising. Prior to Hong Kong, Jon spent a year living in Macau setting up a "Stag-do" business, which he and his business partner still manage. Jon has taken a few breaks during his working life, where he taught English in Granada, Spain, and in Rio de Janeiro. Jon's insights into career breaks and his stories are very entertaining.

Kelly Taylor, client relationship manager, and her husband, both took sabbaticals from their jobs in London and drove to the French Alps to take on the challenging role of managing a chalet. Skiing five days a week was definitely one of their motivators, however, when they were not skiing, some of the work involved in managing a chalet included food shopping and cooking three-course dinners six days per week, sometimes for up to fourteen people plus making cakes for the guest's afternoon tea and cleaning rooms.

Simone Schneider, from Germany, took a three-month career break in 2009. Only one month of her break was unpaid leave, as she utilised her annual leave plus overtime to accumulate her time off. A lover of nature and travelling, Simone jetted to Australia and visited Cairns, then travelled down the east coast to Sydney, then on to the Blue Mountains. Afterwards she flew to New Zealand and did some island hopping in Fiji before stopping in Hong Kong and Macau on the way back to Germany.

Erika Langham worked as a consultant before the global financial crisis saw the work she had lined up for the following year disappear overnight. Taking this as a sign from the universe, she decided to commence her PhD studies on a full-time basis. Whilst still in the early part of this journey, she is enjoying the opportunity to fully immerse herself in her studies, without having to balance them with work demands.

Natalie Shah became acutely aware of the impact the global recession was having on the legal profession in 2009 and watched with dismay as job cuts and redundancies overwhelmed London. Having taken out a loan to fund her legal studies – and with no concrete offer of work in the pipeline—she searched for a way to enhance her CV, increase her employability, and make her application stand out from the competition. After spending three months undertaking a volunteer project in law and human rights in Shanghai, China, with Projects Abroad, she quickly attained a position in a top law firm on her return to London.

Ted Harrington worked in the project management side of construction for over twenty years. A few months after being made redundant, at the age of forty-nine, he climbed Mt Kilimanjaro. Even when faced with altitude sickness and extremely uncomfortable climatic conditions, Ted found himself motivating others to continue to the summit and achieve their goals.

Debbie Norman had always dreamed about sailing on the *Queen Mary 2*, so after spending thirty-five years in banking, she took six months off to fulfil her dream. Debbie returned to work after her break but realised that her aspirations lay elsewhere, and eventually she started her own vintage clothing business. She says her career break and setting up her own business are the best things she's ever done.

Allan Hobart, took his first nine-month sabbatical in 2001 and enjoyed the experience so much he wanted to explore more of the world so took a 3-year career break in 2005, at the age of 33, with a friend who he had met during his sabbatical. After spending 6-months travelling, Allan met his girlfriend (now wife) and they bought a bar together in San Pedro La Laguna, Guatemala, which they successfully ran for two years. Allan also helped out in a school, teaching English to children orphaned by hurricane Stan and also helped build temporary shelters for families who lost their homes.

Gary Davies lives in Somerset, England, and says that after his first break he got hooked. Being an adventurous guy, Gary has done quite a bit of exploring by foot, motorbike, and bicycle. He's visited waterfalls, temples, lakes, and a tiger sanctuary, attended Muay Thai boxing matches, been elephant trekking, rock climbing, quad-biking, boating, and snorkelling.

Simon Ferrier celebrated his forty-fourth birthday whilst volunteering on a deep-sea diving project in Cambodia with Projects Abroad. After being made redundant from the construction industry in December 2009, Simon saw this as an opportunity to take some time out to do something meaningful, which was also his passion, and combine it with travelling through South East Asia.

Rebecca Smith works in the beauty industry and was twenty-three when she took her first career break. She travelled to China, Hong Kong, Laos, Thailand, Malaysia, Singapore, Australia, New Zealand, Fiji, and America. After returning to the UK, she easily slipped straight back into working in beauty. Rebecca's advice to anyone thinking about a career break is, "If you want to do something, just do it."

Helen Norton was working full time as an A&E nurse whilst studying part-time for an MSc in Infrastructure in Emergency. She decided to take a sabbatical from the NHS to get the practical experience she needed for her MSc and thus put theory into practice. This led Helen to Raleigh International to volunteer as a medic and project manager in India.

Richard Nimmo changed his life after volunteering with Blue Ventures on a marine conservation in Madagascar in 2004. He had spent over ten years working in London in sales and marketing for television and radio stations. He felt he needed a break from his hectic and pressurised work life and also had a strong desire to take some time to see and work in a new environment, challenge himself, and make a positive contribution through a conservation project. Richard initially took a three-month break, but instead of returning to his previous work, he gained a position with the volunteering organisation and is now the managing director!

Ann Sullivan was working for an insurance company in Gloucester, UK, when she took her first three-month career break when she travelled through Southeast Asia and India. Ann returned to work, but a year later took voluntary redundancy and quickly planned her next eight-month career break, travelling to Central and South America and Cuba. On her return, Ann completed a TEFL (Teaching English as a Foreign Language) qualification, secured a teaching job in Bangkok.

Euan Platt, a charity youth worker and part-time university student from London, decided that an expedition with Raleigh would benefit his master's degree course. He saw Raleigh as the perfect opportunity for his placement, as it involved working with young people from a range of different backgrounds in a very hands-on way. Euan joined the charity's expedition to Costa Rica and Nicaragua as the team coach and project manager.

Doug Kington, South London, worked in the retail trade. He was twenty-five when he took his first career break, travelling through South America, Borneo, and South East Asia. He returned to England after his break, however, took his second career break due to the economic recession as work opportunities in London were somewhat limited.

Louise Hyde was working very antisocial hours as a doctor in Accident and Emergency. It was a non-training post, and she felt that her career wasn't going anywhere. Louise wanted to learn new skills and build up her self-confidence, and Raleigh seemed to provide the ideal opportunity to achieve these goals. Louise quit her job and joined an expedition as volunteer manager.

Vicky Gardner achieved her dream of being a licensee at the age of twenty-one and hadn't really thought about any further goals. Two years later, her fourteen-year-old brother passed away, and Vicky decided to join her family on their relocation to Australia. This was her first career break, and almost thirteen years later, she is still living in Australia and has since taken another career break. Living the dream and stepping outside her comfort zone are almost daily occurrences. Now Vicky is truly "working to live" and is no longer worried about "living to work"!

Jon Palin volunteered with AVIVA and spent his career break helping SANCCOB to save the lives of penguin chicks and reviewing a fund that helps ensure against natural disasters in the Caribbean. During his travels he indulged his passion for wildlife, seeing the big five (Lion, Rhino, Elephant, Buffalo and Leopard) on safari, cage-diving with great white sharks, and snorkelling with turtles by coral reefs. Since his return he's started to shape a new career mixing consulting, volunteering, and more travel.

Xaali O'Reilly Berkeley had just finished studying and was unsure whether to pursue a future in natural sciences or to become a graphic artist. Uncertain of her future career choices, Xaali took some time out to volunteer overseas. It wasn't long before Xaali found herself in Madagascar, working alongside the locals trying to improve people's livelihoods and stop the ongoing destruction of natural habitats in one of the world's poorest countries.

Christine Hall, a qualified CELTA teacher, returned to the UK after undertaking a volunteer journalism and teaching project in Ethiopia in 2010. She put her house on the market so that she could return to Ethiopia and continue teaching and running an art studio.

Alexis Grant, from Washington, DC, quit her reporting job in 2008 to travel solo through West Africa, Cameroon, and Madagascar. At twenty-seven, she craved the freedom and the challenge—and she knew it was unlikely that her career-minded or family-focused friends would want to accompany her. She is now a travel writer, posting regular articles about her travel experiences on her website.

Alison Light resigned from her job in banking after continually working very long hours. She felt she wasn't experiencing the correct work–life balance. Alison took an eight-month career break, which she spent at home undertaking a variety of activities, including, as she admits, eating lots of cake.

Runa Sadarangani returned from a holiday with a fresh perspective, a newfound enthusiasm, and clarity for what she wanted to do— write a book. She subsequently resigned from her job, booked a writing course in New York and jetted to the Big Apple to fulfil her dream. The course offered her so much more than the framework of how to write a book. It reignited her passion for writing, allowed her the opportunity to meet many like-minded people, and gave her the confidence that she would one day write a book.

Mike Schimanowsky and Kelly Hale packed up their worldly belongings, bade farewell to their friends and family, and traded in their nine-to-five jobs in Canada for a life of nomadic freelancing and travel. Since 2008 Mike and Kelly have travelled to many countries while successfully working in freelance web design/development, and they continue to search for the idyllic stretch of sandy beach … complete with WiFi connection. Mike and Kelly blog about their travels at: http://haveinternetwilltravel.com

Bal Mudhar took a fourteen-month career break in 2005, after taking voluntary redundancy from her job of fifteen years. Firstly, she travelled around Italy, and then spent time with family in the United States and Canada. Following this, she explored much of Australia and overcame a long-held phobia by snorkelling in the open sea. She then explored New Zealand and travelled extensively around Southeast Asia and India before heading home. When Bal returned home it wasn't long before she met her future husband, as a palm reader in Hong Kong had predicted. After a short courtship he proposed, and Bal spent the last few months of her career break planning her wedding.

Jonathan Keevins was working for a Dutch food production company before deciding to volunteer with Raleigh International. After eight years of work, he was keen to take a career break and see a bit of the world. Jonathan joined Raleigh's expedition to Costa Rica & Nicaragua as the Logistics Manager and also volunteered as Expedition Driver and Project Manager.

Tamaryn Dryden took a career break to fulfil her childhood dream of working as a game ranger in her home country of South Africa, before returning to London to continue her career in the field of graduate recruitment. She learnt that working under pressure was when a lion roared five metres behind her, and this has made juggling day-to-day activities a lot easier!

Kate Aston moved to Jersey from London to live with her boyfriend at the beginning of 2009. Her background was in luxury travel; however, not being able to live on the island for more than five years, she was restricted on the jobs she was able to apply for. She ended up juggling three jobs; working in a café; waitressing for an upmarket catering company, and making sausages for a local farmer. Eager for a career break, Katie joined Raleigh's spring expedition in Costa Rica as logistics coordinator and project manager.

Rosie Pebble was sixty-one and considering retirement from her job as a learning support assistant in a comprehensive school in Somerset, England, when she decided to take a career break. Having never been on an aeroplane before, Rosie flew to Romania to do voluntary work in a hospital and orphanage.

Special Thanks

A number of people within the career break and volunteer organisation community were very supportive and helpful when I was conducting my research. My gratitude extends to:

- Sophie Pell, Raleigh International
- Koreen Walsh, Projects Abroad
- Jeff Jung, Career Break Secrets
- Ed Scott, AVIVA, South Africa
- Mark Jacobs, Azafady
- Richard Nimmo, Blue Ventures
- Sherry Ott, Briefcase to Backpack
- Alexis Grant, The Travelling Writer

SOME LIGHT READING

Listed below, you'll find a host of websites that will provide you with information on a variety of career break sites, travel companies, volunteer organizations, TEFL providers, and the like. Most of these have been referenced during the book to aid you in your research. I hope you find the experience you are looking for!

Career Break Sites and Information

- **Career Break Secrets** – www.careerbreaksecrets.com
- **Yoursabbatical.com** – www.yoursabbatical.com
- **The Career Break Site** – www.thecareerbreaksite.com
- **Career Break Café** – www.careerbreakcafe.com
- **Gap Year for Grown Ups** – www.gapyearforgrownups. co.uk
- **A Career Break** – www.acareerbreak.co.uk
- **i-to-i Volunteer and Adventure Travel** – www.i-to-i.com/career-break-resources
- **Gap Work** – www.gapwork.com/career-break.shtml
- **Indie Travel Podcast** – www.indietravelpodcast.com
- **Alexis Grant, The Travel Writer** – www.alexisgrant.com

Career Break Specialists

- **Briefcase to Backpack** – www.b2b.meetplango.com
- **Meet, Plan, Go!** – www.meetplango.com
- **Three Month Visa** – www.threemonthvisa.com

Booking Your Flights and Some Tours

- **Trailfinders** – www.trailfinders.com
- **Flight Centre** – www.flightcentre.com
- **Expedia** – www.expedia.com
- **Round the World Experts** – www.roundtheworldexperts.co.uk

Volunteer Organisations

- **Raleigh International** – www.raleighinternational.org
- **Projects Abroad** – www.projects-abroad.co.uk
- **Ecoteer** – www.ecoteer.com
- **AVIVA** – www.aviva-sa.com
- **Blue Ventures** – www.blueventures.org
- **VSO** – www.vso.org.uk
- **UN** – www.unv.org
- **Inspire** – www.inspirekenya.com/Inspirekenya.com
- **i-to-i Volunteer and Adventure Travel** – www.i-to-i.com
- **Kaya Volunteer** – www.kayavolunteer.com
- **Mondo Challenge** – www.mondochallenge.co.uk
- **Year Out Gap** – www.yearoutgap.org
- **Action Without Borders** – www.idealist.org
- **Worldwide Volunteering** – www.worldwidevolunteering.org
- **World Service Enquiry** – www.wse.org.uk
- **Mad Adventurers** – www.madventurer.com
- **Volunteer Latin America** – www.volunteerlatinamerica.com
- **Azafady** – www.madagascar.co.uk
- **World-Wide Volunteering** – www.wwv.org.uk
- **Open Mind Projects** – www.openmindprojects.org

- **U Volunteering** – www.uvolunteer.org
- **Ecoteer** – www.ecoteer.com
- **Volunteer Work Thailand** – www.volunteerworkthailand.org
- **Volunteer 4 Africa** – www.volunteer4africa.org

Responsible Tourism and CBT

- **Responsible Travel** – www.responsibletravel.com/copy/responsible-tourism
- **Responsible Tourism Awards** – www.responsibletourismawards.com
- **Nutty's Adventures** – www.nutty-adventures.com
- **Intrepid Travel** – www.intrepidtravel.com/responsibletravel
- **Voluntourism** – www.voluntourism.co.uk

Companies Offering a Variety of Adventure Travel

- **Activities Abroad, the Activity Travel Company** – www.activitiesabroad.com
- **Exodus** – www.exodus.co.uk
- **Imaginative Traveller** – www.imaginative-traveller.com
- **Gap Adventures** – www.gapadventures.com
- **Yomps** – www.yomps.co.uk

Companies Offering a Variety of Comfort Travel

- **Intrepid Travel** – www.intrepidtravel.com
- **Comfort Travel (Canada)** – www.comforttravel.ca
- **Discover China Tours** – www.discoverchinatours.com
- **Comfort Safaris** – www.comfortsafaris.com

Companies Offering a Variety of Budget Travel

- **Intrepid Travel** – www.intrepidtravel.com
- **Gecko's Adventures** – www.geckosadventures.com
- **Real Gap** – www.realgap.co.uk
- **Gap Year** – www.gapyear.com

Companies Offering a Variety of Family Travel

- **Intrepid Travel** – www.intrepidtravel.com
- **Peregrine Adventures** – www.peregrineadventures.com
- **Adventure Company** – www.adventurecompany.co.uk
- **Travelmood Adventures** – www.travelmoodadventures.com

TEFL Courses

- **TEFL** – www.tefl.com
- **i-to-i Volunteer and Travel Abroad** – www.i-to-i.com/tefl
- **ihBangkok** – www.ihbangkok.com
- **International Teacher Training Organisation** – www.teflcertificatecourses.com/specials
- **TEFL courses offered in Australia** – www.teflcertificationabroad.com/search/australia

Working Abroad Websites

- **Working Abroad Magazine** – www.workingabroadmagazine.com

Courses and Seminars—America

- **Media Bistro** – www.mediabistro.com/courses

Online Freelance Websites

- **Elance** – www.elance.com
- **Peopleperhour** – www.peopleperhour.com
- **Weedle** – www.weedle.com
- **oDesk** – www.odesk.com

Family Travels Websites

- **Home School Blogger** – www.homeschoolblogger.com/rvhomeschool
- **Away We Go. US** – www.awaywego.us/homeschool.html
- **abc7** - www.abclocal.go.com/kabc/story?section=news/local/ventura_county&id=6594362

Finances

- **The Careerbreakcafe.com** – www.careerbreakcafe.com/career-break-money
- **Gapadvice.org** – www.gapadvice.org/career-breaks/finance
- **i-to-i Volunteer and Adventure Travel** – www.i-to-i.com/how-to-manage-your-money
- **U.S. News & World Report** – www.money.usnews.com/money/personal-finance/articles/2011/05/25/can-i-afford-to-take-a-sabbatical)

And here are a few books:

King, S. & Robertson, E. (2004). *The Backpacker's Bible* (4th ed.). Robson Books.

Lansky, D. (2003). *First-Time around the World: A Trip Planner for the Ultimate Journey.* Rough Guide.

Griffiths, S. (2008). *Gap Year for Grown Ups* (3rd edition). Crimson Publishing.

Griffiths, T. (2003). *Before You Go* (3rd ed.). Bloomsbury Publishing.

I shall leave you with a couple of quotes. The first from Simon Calder, TV presenter and travel editor of The Independent Newspaper, United Kingdom.

> "The principal job of the career break is that it allows you to look at the world afresh, to un-cloud your mind and your eyes and focus on what really matters to you. For most of us, that means family and friends. But whether you're 1,000 miles or 10,000 miles from home, thoughts from abroad bring a clarity of emotion to these relationships. And, it also allows you the time to conclude that yes, you do deserve to take a pause from the industrious life you have pursued."
>
> (Independent travel, Wanderlust: *Guide to Career Breaks*, p. 6)

And, finally, one from me!

> If you don't take a chance in life, how are you going to experience anything different?

ABOUT THE AUTHOR

Sue Hadden has taken two career breaks over the last six years spending her time travelling to the United States, through South East Asia and Australia. During her breaks Sue experimented with new careers possibilities (some successfully, some unsuccessfully), made new friends, learnt new skills, spent time with her family and friends, completed a professional qualification and attended a host of workshops, retreats and conferences.

During her second 18-month career break, Sue trained as a professional coach. Given the positive impact of her own experiences, Sue combined her passion of career breaks with her desire to help make a difference in people's lives and wrote this book to inspire others to do the same.

Not only does Sue share the trials, tribulations and experiences of her own career breaks, other 'career breakers' Sue has either met on her travels or approached while writing the book, have contributed their own stories bringing the book to life. You can read about volunteering, freelancing, studying, renovating a property, travelling, budgeting, how to ask for a career break and so much more. Sue also interviewed industry experts who shared their career break commentary, opinions and guidance on the value of taking a career break and how it can positively affect your life in so many ways.

Sue is Australian by birth and spent over 11 years living in London before moving to New York. She is a qualified NLP Practitioner and has worked in the financial services industry for over 13 years. The skills and knowledge Sue developed during her career breaks have allowed her to move forward in her career, including an international transfer, where she is able to live her purpose in life every day – to lead and inspire others.